A FATHER'S DAUGHTER

STEPHEN BRADLEY-WATERS

Copyright © 2019 Stephen Bradley-Waters

All rights reserved.

ISBN: 9781701416260

DEDICATION

For my beautiful daughter.

CONTENTS

INTRODUCTION		7
1	THE BEGINNING	9
2	JESSIE	14
3	ABDUCTION	17
4	PSYCHIC	21
5	INNOCENCE	28
6	TRAUMA	31
7	FIRST CONTACT	36
8	ARGUMENT	42
9	DEPRESSION	51
10	FIRST COURT HEARING	55
11	SUMMER 2017	59
12	CANCER	64
13	DISRUPTION	67
14	CASEY	72
15	SECOND COURT HEARING	80
16	THIRD COURT HEARING	89
17	THREE HOUR CONTACT	97
18	FIVE HOUR CONTACT	111
19	FOURTH COURT HEARING	122
20	PREPARATION	128
21	FIFTH COURT HEARING	134
22	RETURNING HOME	141
23	R.I.P.	154
24	MENTAL HEALTH	159
25	NOVEMBER CONTACT	172
26	FUNERAL	184
27	CONFUSION	187
28	THE NEW YEAR	195
29	CHILD ABUSE	201
30	TRAVEL ARRANGEMENTS	212
31	FLIGHTS	221
32	CAFCASS OFFICER	225
33	EASTER	230
34	DE-JA-VU	235
35	MAY DAY	240
36	PRESSURE	243
37	EMOTIONAL COURT	248

38 GUARDIAN BATTLE	255
39 SUMMER HOLIDAY	258
40 AFTER HOLIDAYS	262
41 A FINAL HURRAH	266
42 FINAL – DAY ONE	268
43 FINAL – DAY TWO	282
CONCLUSION	288
EPILOGUE – PART ONE	290
EPILOGUE – PART TWO	301
FINAL THOUGHT	304
APPENDIX	305
ACKNOWLEDGEMENTS	309
ABOUT THE AUTHOR	312

AUTHOR'S NOTE

It has been an emotional journey writing this book — my first foray into professional writing. A life goal fulfilled. I would, however, rather not have this story to tell. Reliving the past and opening old wounds have been tormenting on the mind. A massive event in my life that I felt compelled to retell. This book will make sharing my story easier, rather than continuously repeating myself.

Some chapters were harder than others to relive. I often found myself on a sound momentum of writing. Everything was coming thick and fast. Then there were moments I didn't want to remember. I didn't want to face again. So, the book was left for weeks at a time. In one instance, I didn't come back to writing it for over a month. It meant too much to me not to finish. Eventually, I sat down and wrestled with my demons to get this story told. As a strange coincidence, I finished writing A Father's Daughter on would you believe - Father's Day 2019.

This is a moment in my life that I would like to leave behind. Forget and move on, and never look back. The mind won't allow that, though. Too much has happened. These moments will forever be a significant part of my life. Growing up, I never thought in my wildest dreams that I would endure such turmoil. Appear in front of a judge and fight for my life in court.

I'm proud of my efforts in and out of court and finding the grit and willpower to finish writing this book.

Something that started with a simple blank page would become one of my most significant accomplishments. I dared to be brave and reach for the stars. It wasn't easy, and nothing worth achieving is. Here I am pouring my heart out, sharing a moment in my history and a time of courage and struggle, fighting for someone I hold most dear in my life - my daughter.

I have tried to recreate events, locales, and conversations from my memories of them. To maintain their anonymity in some instances, I have changed the names of individuals and places. I may have changed some identifying characteristics and details such as physical properties, occupations and places of residence.

COURT

Family Courts in the UK are suffering from an unprecedented number of superficial claims of abuse against innocent people for someone's sole purpose of gaining free public funding (legal aid) towards their legal costs. Meanwhile, the other person faces an uphill battle for justice at an incredible loss in the tens of thousands of pounds while having their character tainted as an abuser.

Prior to 2013 legal aid was available to low-income applicants. The law changed limiting legal aid only to victims of abuse, which opened an increase in claims of this nature.

There are many failures within the legal system in the present state which has far-reaching consequences to innocent people not involved within the legal proceedings. Places in refuge accommodation are limited. Real victims of abuse are struggling to find a way out of their traumatic situations as space they so desperately need within a refuge has been taken up by so many false victims.

As it currently stands anyone can claim to be in an abusive relationship and get protection from various agencies such as Women's Aid who support them with placement in a refuge, applying for and endorsing a claim for legal aid, fast track to housing and a grant to furnish the property. There's a lot to gain in claiming abuse.

INTRODUCTION

Finally arriving home after the drive south from the gusty north-west was a huge relief. The journey had been long and exhausting — more than 200 miles of treacherous dimly lit roads. The night sky consumed everything in its wake. Visibility reduced to just the car lights in front. Now and then a speeding car would over-take in the outside lane, providing some respite from the darkness with a sudden glimmer of light, disappearing just as fast as it came. The drive was a grind with so many thoughts racing through my mind. The road just went on and on with no end in sight. My mind consumed in deep thought, dissecting everything that had happened earlier that day.

With the flick of a switch, the headlights powered off. A journey complete. Arriving alone didn't feel right. Something was missing. Walking along the path to my home was a lonely and isolating experience. Entering the flat didn't feel any better. An empty kids' bedroom was ominously missing a child. A room, waiting and wanting company. Toys ready to be played with, TV prepared to show a movie — everything waiting to be used. Today I feel just as empty as the room itself. All hope faded away. It wasn't the welcome home I had expected. It was a day to forget.

It had taken eighteen months to get to this moment. A shocking amount of time considering the urgency of the situation. I have much to understand and comprehend. A lot has happened with no time to take it all in. This book is a documentation of everything that has transpired.

1

THE BEGINNING

From an early age, I always knew that becoming a father was incredibly important to me. Deep down, I'm sure my father abandoning me as a child was the catalyst. Mum went on to marry Michael, who had three boys of his own. Add this to the four children already in our family. We now totalled seven children, two girls, and five boys. He would become an incredible role-model — someone to look up to and be inspired by. My stepdad placed family above everything. Taught all of us to stick together and be there for one another. He led by example. Always available for anything any of us ever needed.

It's corny to say that if I become half the man he was, then I would count myself lucky. However, that is so true. Not only did he inspire me, but all my siblings, our children, and their children. We lost him to a long battle with cancer months into my daughter's abduction and contributed significantly towards the legal costs in my pursuit to bring her home. Even in the last moments of his life family remained his absolute priority. There was a large attendance of people mourning him at his funeral, which demonstrated the respect, so many people had for him — an unassuming hero.

Casey kept so many secrets from friends and family. She suffers severely with her mental health, diagnosed with depression, severe anxiety, and obsessive-compulsive disorder — a cocktail of issues culminating in dangerous circumstances. Every day was unique, sometimes good though other-times bad. She hid a lot of her feelings behind a fake smile. Most people wouldn't see the suffering, but I could always tell the difference between a happy or sad Casey. She is incredibly vulnerable, requiring plenty of support and guidance. The depression makes her moods low and fragile. The anxiety makes her impulsive and dangerous. The OCD adds to her frustrations, which can be the catalyst that pushes her over the edge.

I had supported Casey throughout our relationship. As the years went on, Casey's mood fluctuated severely up and down. I cared for her and encouraged the best I could. The weight of responsibility and the feeling of being trapped eventually took a toll on me. Life had become a roadblock with no potential for any progression with a career as I felt responsible for caring for her. I didn't resent Casey as she meant the world to me, but something was missing in my life. I am ambitious and dream of being a success to fulfil my potential and be an inspiration to my daughter Jessie. It wasn't a sacrifice to not pursue my dreams as in many ways, I was already living the best part of that dream. Spending time with my family and making sure they are all safe and cared for was my absolute priority.

At thirty-four years old, the most difficult moments of my life were to come. While the preceding two years were incredibly difficult for a multitude of reasons, 2017 was to be the worst year of my life. In 2015 Casey and I were evicted from our privately rented home. The landlord wanted to sell the property. We tried in vain to contest the eviction through the court. We were successful in delaying the outcome; however, it was inevitable for us to leave eventually. As the new year began, we had no choice but to reside at my parents' small bungalow with the children. With limited rooms and space, the only option was to sleep behind the sofa. It wasn't comfortable and very difficult for all parties. Casey took this especially hard as her family wouldn't accommodate her or the children. She craved the freedom we had once cherished by living on our own. There were more issues she contended with though that's not for now. We endured this living arrangement for nine months.

Eventually, we found new accommodation in the autumn of 2015. Our local council provided us with accommodation after a very lengthy application process. Initially, Casey refused to accept the new property. I was shocked. The property had a no dogs policy which Casey declined. I'm not heartless, I also adored our pets, but the kid's lives were much more critical. If we must let the pets go to a new home, then it is a sacrifice worth making. I felt that Casey was placing the animals above the children. They loved the dogs too, but time is a healer, and they would've been fine.

I had no choice but to speak with the housing manager at Chelmsford council to try in vain to get pets allowed at the property. To help sway the situation in our favour, I explained Casey's issues and her attachment to the animals. A positive outcome negotiated between the manager and I. We were now allowed two dogs. It was made clear to me that that is the absolute limit. We would need to re-home one of them. I felt victorious. My positive mood quickly took a turn for the worst when I explained everything to Casey. She was adamant that she wouldn't go without all the dogs.

I couldn't believe what I heard - selfishness without any care for the children. They don't have any personal space or a room of their own. It's imperative that they have their own home. Animals don't live as long as people, and they soon get attached to new families. I couldn't get her to see common sense. She was adamant that the dogs were too important. It was shocking to witness. Without going into too much detail, she had become a danger to herself as she couldn't cope with the current living situation. I knew her mind was fragile and delicate. It was imperative that we have a home so she can recover and gain a positive outlook on life.

We accepted the property but had to make sure we kept one dog hidden at all times. More hassle than it's worth and didn't help with settling into our new home. We were always nervous about getting caught. It's a violation of the terms of the tenancy. If found to be in breach, we would face eviction. I wasn't happy with the situation at all, but I couldn't do anything other than support Casey.

The children were delighted, and we made the new place feel like home. For a while, we were all satisfied and contemplated a positive future. It didn't take long for Casey's mood to drop. Her desires failed to align with that of my own. I tried to accommodate and support everything she ever wanted. Over-time my efforts weren't enough for her. In reality, it never was - merely delaying the inevitable.

Casey had a history of becoming bored with people and her surroundings. Relationships were often short-lived and rather fleeting. She would find the ending of relationships difficult to the point where she would often flee many miles away. Before our courtship, her daughter, Emma, had been left in the care of the grandparents for three months and no contact with the father. They were shocked as she was only supposed to have gone for a weekend. It's this impulsive and selfish behaviour which scares me the most. She has done it before and is now repeating it.

2

JESSIE

At the now age of seven, Jessie's birth feels so long ago. The little things remain locked into memory like time capsules, though the details surrounding those events fade into the distance. Taking her home from the hospital for the very first time was exciting and nerve-wracking. Knowing how delicate she is and feeling a sense of protecting her in a bubble to shield her from the world still resonates to this day.

As an overly protective parent, she knows to hold my hand as we walk along the street and through crowds of people. The thought of anything happening to this precious angel bare not contemplating. Of course, as she gets older, the urge to protect will be outweighed by the necessity to provide her with the freedom to explore and develop her individuality.

The balance and transition won't be as smooth as one would prefer and of course, not of one's choosing. There are two parents of whom have a say in her upbringing, and there's also Jessie's own wishes to consider. A fact I'm expecting to hear all too often as she reaches adolescence. A possible rebellion may be in the offing.

An infectious smile compliments her adorable and

charming personality - free-spirited, full of joy and playfulness. She is both funny and compassionate. Doesn't like to see other people suffering and feels a sense of protectiveness to younger, more vulnerable children. She is approachable without arrogance — an impressive upgrade from both mother and father.

Almost all parents feel a sense of adjuration and love for their children, and if they didn't, that would be rather worrying. I will love my daughter through any flaws and mishaps that may befall her though I feel as though I got fortunate and hit the jackpot.

How this beautiful girl with impeccable morals and charm could be created is remarkable, and in part by me is even more peculiar. To start with, I have the singing voice of a donkey being chocked and spanked at the same time. Jessie has an angelic voice which she could potentially develop and who knows what the future will bring for her. She has so many positive facets to her personality that the possibilities are endless.

I have been known to have fleeting moments of randomness with complete disregard for other people's opinions on how my behaviour appears — a goofball which Jessie enjoys. Smiling from ear to ear she makes me want to be that man-child much like Peter Pan and whisk her off to Neverland.

There are some moments when we are very much like that. In a field only recently, we played sorcery with sticks as wands casting spells upon each other and those around us as if we were characters from Harry Potter. Pretending to ride horses, we would gallop and race through the wide-open fields laughing with joy. These moments do happen, and they aren't in some made up stories. The world around us can be rather unforgiving. It's essential to take the time to have fun and transcend from reality if only for a short while.

3

ABDUCTION

April 24, 2017, is a day etched into memory. It was to be the worst day of my life. I had spent the night alone while my daughter and her half-sister had a sleepover at their grandparents' home with their mother. The relationship between Casey and I had been in severe decline for many months. The strain of being in proximity to one another became a cause of irritation. After almost eight years of living together, life had become monotonous. The past few weeks had been very fractious with many heated arguments about our living arrangements, family and petty differences.

I awoke early at 6.30am. My initial thought was Jessie. Spending a night away from her isn't something that comes easy as we are very rarely apart. I had remembered that DVD's were in her school bag. A text message was sent to Casey, thus reminding her to remove the movies before Jessie leaves for school.

Me: Don't forget to take the DVDs out of Jessie's bag.

A further message was sent at 9.45am.
Me: Did they get to school, OK?

Casey responded almost immediately.

A FATHER'S DAUGHTER

Casey: Yes, they are at school :)

The children were due to spend two nights at the grandparents' home to provide Casey, and I time apart. We had agreed the previous day that I would call to speak to the children at 6 pm each evening. Sunday hadn't gone according to plan. Phone calls were unresponsive, which was a cause of frustration. Two hours later than agreed the call finally connected and I had a short conversation with Jessie. It was evident that she was having a movie night and enjoying the change of environment though she was slightly missing home.

I reluctantly decided not to have a conversation with Emma. It had become evident over the past few weeks that she had been manipulated and becoming more distant and ruder. Jessie would remain with me when Casey absconded weekends though Emma stayed with the grandparents much to my protests. I saw no benefit in us speaking while she is in their care as they heavily influence her.

Tonight, we remain apart as arranged one more time before she is due to return home. I decided to try and call earlier as it may be easier to speak to Jessie just after school as opposed to a busy evening. Over four hours of phone call attempts remained unanswered. Confused, I couldn't understand why there was no response. In-between phone calls text messages were sent in the hope that it will prompt a response.

The following message sent at 4.38pm.

Me: Can you call me when Jessie's free to chat so I can

hear how her days been.

A few minutes later, another message sent.
Me: Tried phoning but appears as though your phone is off.

A final message was sent at 5.54pm providing an intended time to call.
Me: I'll phone again at 7 as planned, figured would've been easier for her to speak earlier.

I was utterly bewildered by the lack of response from Casey. She is obsessed with her phone, so it's doubtful that she can't read the messages or notice the calls. It didn't make any sense that she was ignoring me. We were polite and amicable the previous day when Casey and the children left for their two-night stay-over at Casey's parents. As Casey was going, she was happy and said "Bye, see you soon" to which I responded, "Have fun".

9 pm and still no response to the calls. Knowing how connected Casey is to her phone, I was very concerned. If the phone battery needed charging it would have finished by now. Maybe she's gone for a day out shopping or has something happened?

Concerned, I phoned my mother, Genine. I informed her of the lack of any response to the messages or calls. Mum was equally confused as she also knew Casey as being very attached to her phone. I asked if she could try calling Casey to see if there's a dial tone as I wasn't getting anything from my phone.

The call ended so that my mum can attempt to call Casey. To my astonishment, she informed me that she had heard a dial tone, but then it stopped. Upon trying to call again, there was no connection. It was evident that she had blocked my number and now my mother's too. The big question was why? I don't obsessively message or call, so it's unnecessary.

Suddenly, an overwhelming feeling of dread and fear consumed me. It dawned on me that Casey has done it, she has taken our daughter!

4

PSYCHIC

My life was in turmoil with so much uncertainty — an emotional mess consumed with a feeling of dread and loss. Mum knew a few local psychics. Arrangements were scheduled for me to have a tarot card reading with a lady named Sal at my parents' home. I'm sceptical though have an open mind.

The beauty of life is the unknown of what will happen next. It's a mystery. For life to be planned out in advance would lose the thrill of living it and have the potential to be boring. Now I'm at crossroads, feeling lost — void of hope or understanding of my current circumstances. There was no better time than now to know what my future has in store for me.

As soon as the psychic reading commenced, it felt as though Sal understood what I was going through without having to be told — immediately understanding my circumstances and the problems endured. She emphasised, "You are stuck without any control while everything is going on around you".

I had never thought of my current predicament in that way, but it made perfect sense. Regardless of what I did, it made no difference to anything. That one comment stayed in my head for a long time after and remains with me still to this day. It gave me a sense of peace and tranquillity amongst the mayhem that ensued — realising that so much is beyond my control — allowing me to relax in moments when I otherwise would've been on edge and anxious.

It was evident to Sal that the current issue plighting me and causing incredible distress is the ending of a relationship and separation from my daughter. It was a very recent event, so I was shocked that she knew. Sal recognised that Casey has issues, stating that "She's not all there" a reference to being slightly crazy. I confirmed that as being correct.

Sal was adamant that I would see Jessie soon. She couldn't confirm when but was comfortable telling me that it will happen. There are a lot of lies and deceit from Casey and her mother. She warned that I couldn't afford to slip up even once. I had to be perfect throughout proceedings; otherwise, it will all go against me. Playing into their hands as they try to set me up as something that I'm not.

She asked if I have the women solicitors or the man, suggesting that women will do well. That was pleasing as I do have an all women legal team supporting me.

Casey is in a secret relationship though Sal was adamant that it wouldn't last. She didn't specify for how long or why it would fail, but she was absolute in her confirmation. I hadn't been sure whether Casey had been visiting her cousin as she had suggested or seeing someone behind my back. My solicitors and family felt that she had been cheating, but I didn't want to believe that. Hearing it from an impartial person with apparent psychic abilities was the confirmation I needed to accept the infidelity and move on.

There was a suggestion that Casey is either taking drugs or abusing alcohol. I felt it unlikely though maybe the drinking as she enjoyed getting smashed weekends before our relationship. With her now solely responsible for both children though I think perhaps Sal is referencing her medication as she has a few different pills to help her cope with her issues. That could be the reference to drugs. It doesn't always have to be sinister.

Sal emphasised, 'You need always to be one step ahead of her. It is imperative.' I had already started to gather evidence in preparation for an almost certain custody battle through the courts. Her prophecy was already well underway as I put my heart and soul into doing everything to get my daughter home. No stone was being left unturned. I was relentless.

The topic of court proceedings was very insightful. A suggestion that the court would conclude within 6-7 weeks. Full custody of my daughter won't be for another 7-8 months. This conflicting information confused me. Even to this day, I try to understand the significance of what she means. How can the court conclude within weeks but not get custody for nearly a year later? That made no sense to me. 'You don't have to give in to any of her demands' of this Sal was certain. She knew the battle between us would be brutal and not without sacrifice and heartache, but I must remain strong. Eventually, Casey will give up the fight. Again, this was vague. Give up through court? After court? Give up fighting me? Or give up trying to hold our daughter against her wishes? It could be anything at any moment. All I can do is the right things and hope that one day at some point, my daughter can come home to me.

'Casey isn't interested in your shared tenancy flat. It's yours if I want it.' She won't be coming back were the words I didn't want to hear. I had hoped in my heart that her recent actions were an impulsive decision she would instantly regret and return home to me where she is loved and adored. To hear that it won't be happening was soul-crushing and destroyed me inside — the life I had loved gone forever.

'You won't want anything to do with Casey and have absolutely no feelings for her.' I was at a loss. Over the many years in our relationship, Casey had been trying and unpredictable, but I never felt at any moment that I would hate her to the point of not caring. Even in the moments, I suffer the love I have for her is immense. To lose that love, she would have to push me to hell and back. Something I don't think she would do. She's not that nasty. Selfish at times, yes but not vengeful. I wasn't so sure about me not having any feelings for her. Doesn't seem possible, although everyone has their breaking point. Can only tolerate so much before the charm is gone and replaced with darker feelings of hate.

There was a strong feeling from Sal that Casey's family underestimate me. In all likelihood, they were comparing me to Emma's dad who doesn't have anywhere near the same commitment towards his daughter as I do mine. That would be their downfall as nothing will stop me pursuing my daughter's happiness and assuming my rightful place within her life. If they felt I would quit because it gets too complicated or expensive, they were wrong.

"Your daughter will be in a hospital." were the words that overshadowed everything. I froze and felt an incredible sense of uneasiness. Of course, the worst-case scenarios immediately came to mind. Then the thought of her needing to be there can't be good whatever the reason. I questioned the validity, but Sal was sure of it. It made me more desperate than ever to get Jessie home now.

The next topic wasn't any better. There will be a funeral. Sal wouldn't elaborate on who's funeral but that there will be one. My stepdad had been fighting a battle with cancer for a few years but seemed to be doing fine so apart from him I couldn't think of who it could be. Whoever it is it would be terrible. It played on my mind for a while after the reading. Who on earth could it be?

There won't be any new relationships for the foreseeable future as I'm not in that place in my mind yet though a Jenny will come back into my life. This confused, as I didn't know a Jenny that I could recall. I had known a Holly from a few years ago before my relationship with Casey. I think maybe she saw the double letters in a name as opposed to a specific name. That's the only way to make sense of it without dismissing it altogether.

One part of the reading was unconvincing, which if wrong casts doubts on all of it. Sal said, "You will see your natural father, not this one here as he's not your natural father, is he?" she pointed at the empty sofa where my stepdad usually sits. We had the reading while he was out as he doesn't believe in psychics or anything paranormal. "You'll receive money from him". She was in no doubt, no matter how many times I made it clear that I was genuinely not interested in seeing him. I explained that I'm not one of those people that say one thing but secretly want to. My stepdad raised me all my life alongside my mum and siblings; this is my family.

My natural father is no more than a sperm donor in my eyes. I don't hold any regret, anger or feel vengeful. It's simply that my family is large enough as it is. To wait until I'm in my thirties to get in touch is pointless. I have a child of my own now. I don't need a dad to care or love me. I am a dad. My time as a child finished a long time ago. There's only one way I could envisage seeing him. If it was on his death bed and it was a dying wish. I'm not so cold-hearted that I would deny someone closure for something they may want to make amends finally. I've heard from my mum and sisters that he has many more children of his own. I'm the eldest boy, but he has another life now. I had a brief look at his social media and Linkedin profile, which portrayed him as having a successful career. We did communicate via email briefly a few years ago. He wanted to meet while I didn't. He stated that he had reconciled with his other children. They shared a few tears. I made it clear that there would be no tears from me as I don't feel emotional about what happened. My mum raised me well in his absence.

Money was a sore spot in my life at this moment in time. Debts mounting from my bills and those Casey left behind, getting worse as each week goes by. My mind wasn't in a place capable of addressing them anytime soon. What's the point when everything in my life was gone. "Although your financial situation is difficult, you will be OK." were Sal's comforting words, though there doesn't seem to be an end in sight. Just more problems on top of the previous. Debt after debt continually increasing.

Who knows what the future has in store but it's not something I spend any amount of time dwelling. My priority is my daughter.

5

INNOCENCE

The bond between Jessie and I has been incredibly strong from the moment she was born. I had never been so proud of something or someone in my entire life. I was concerned that Jessie might be born with medical defects. My partner Casey is a carrier of a low immune system genetic condition. The worry wasn't that my life would be challenging to manage with the added problems. It's that I wanted the best possible life for Jessie.

It became apparent early on in Jessie's life that she had skin issues. Her skin would flare up and become hot and itchy. Our dog, Daisy, was reluctantly re-homed as her hair made Jessie's condition worse. I suffer from dry skin, and Casey has eczema so it shouldn't have come as a surprise. Jessie's skin is manageable by only using medicated skin care products while avoiding traditional hand-washes and bath soaps. Keeping her away from heat for extended periods is also beneficial. Once the skin flares, it becomes worse as she can't help but itch, which can cause infections and more irritability.

As babies tend to be up in the night causing havoc crying, I would care for Jessie through the night providing her with a bottle, nappy changes and entertain her when it was required while Casey slept. I'd also ease her back to sleep when the opportunity presented itself as she also needed her rest.

Playing with her and watching her grow and develop was a great source of enjoyment for me. I would often play peek-a-boo with her through her crib and cot, lay and interact with her. Jessie's development and sense of being loved was and is hugely important to me.

I taught and encouraged Jessie doing my best to support her, whether it be crawling, standing, walking or speaking. Compared to Jessie's half-sister Emma at three years old, Jessie's speech was a lot clearer. I had spent my time nurturing Jessie, whereas Emma didn't get that support from her father. When he arrived to collect Emma, he often struggled to understand what she was trying to say.

I encouraged Jessie to share toys as selfishness and being spoilt isn't a trait I wanted instilling into her mindset from an early age. It was important to me that she be modest, approachable and kind-hearted. She would go on to be all these things and more — a genuinely amazing kindhearted person.

Jessie's achievements astounded me and filled my heart with so much pride. Witnessing her stand supported holding onto something was a significant milestone. As was her doing the same thing unaided, crawling, walking and speaking it all blew me away. She was growing and developing in front of my eyes.

Between two and three years old, she was and is the case with most toddlers a handful. She would growl and get angry; it was a rather tiring time in her development. Testing boundaries and limits were a regular occurrence. I provided a consistent discipline structure, so Jessie grew to develop an understanding of the behaviour expected of her. It was vital that she be respectful and considerate of others. Understand that no means no and as her speech developed to ask for things with manners. Please and thank you don't cost anything but make a huge difference when interacting with people.

6

TRAUMA

My beautiful and funny child had been taken away from me without warning. For the first time in her life, I couldn't protect, reassure or show her the love in my heart. Only a few days before this event she was so full of joy and excitement for her upcoming birthday. While mummy and daddy had heated conversations about their relationship, Jessie would be curious "Are you talking about my birthday?" to which we would reply, "Yes".

Her little face would light up with intrigue. Little did Jessie or I know all those plans we had in store for her birthday were not to be. She'd instead spend her time in a refuge without her father knowing where she was, how long they would be away, and who she's with (aside from her mother and sister).

The thought of Jessie being somewhere so unfamiliar away from family and friends breaks my heart every day. A child so compassionate and thoughtful of others is in the care of someone who's main thought is themselves. A severe injustice has happened to this innocent soul. More than anything daddy wants to protect her, bring her home and let her know how much he cherishes her. Play, have fun and make her happy. But for all Jessie knows daddy doesn't care, he hasn't come to help, and he missed her birthday.

Since the day Jessie was taken away by someone I had loved and trusted, I have been restless in my pursuit to bring her home. Trying Casey's family and friends were met with complete ignorance. No-one would respond to messages. Casey had blocked all communications. I was lost, anxious, and completely isolated from my daughter. Being away from Jessie doesn't come easy. I often cry every-time I think of her. She's the light in my life, makes me so proud. We have a very close bond with very similar personalities. Playing and laughing is effortless between us. Doing nothing and waiting to see what happens is not an option.

With so many thoughts racing through my mind. Where could Casey have taken her? Why has she taken her? What does she expect to gain from it? How long will they be gone? It was easy to feel wholly negative and helpless. Instead, I harnessed the negative and used it to do something positive. Contacted the police to check on the welfare of Jessie. It took three days of phone calls. The last call on Wednesday 26th April 2017 had me in a phone call queue for 1 hour. Finally, the case was assigned to a sergeant. A voicemail was received before 4 pm stating they have been found and are safe and well. This put my mind was put at ease; however, the sergeant wouldn't disclose their location. So now she could still be anywhere. In an unfamiliar place, surrounded by unknown people without her dad to reassure her. Throughout this ordeal, I kept in contact with the school to keep them up to date and find out if they had heard anything or whether the kids have returned.

With my mum for support, we visited Citizens Advice to get informed of my legal rights. Phoning and visiting solicitors we were told that legal aid had been abolished. We then made an appointment to see the solicitor that had previously dealt with my brother David's custody battle a year or two prior.

I actively got to work building my legal case by retrieving plenty of evidence to support my claim for custody. Letters were sent to the school and Casey's parents stating that we are actively seeking to find and speak with her about the care of Jessie. If that fails, then a court summons will be the next step; however, finding Casey was imperative to serve her with the papers.

In the meantime, my solicitors had found out on the 4th May 2017 via the sergeant who had dealt with my case the previous week that Casey had placed herself and the kids in a refuge., which completely broke my heart. I was inconsolable in floods of tears. How could she take the kids out of school to a place they don't know when they could've been home? I was forced to miss Jessie's birthday, which I had never happened before. Completely distraught, I couldn't understand how someone could be so cruel as to divide a child from their parent on such an important day of her life. A moment we will never get back. Her birthday presents and card remained at home waiting for her return.

On the day I found out that Jessie was in a refuge, I discussed possible scenarios for Casey to have gone to it with my solicitor and family. It was apparent she had done so to give herself leverage on either trying to legally take over the tenancy of our shared tenancy flat, try to get legal aid for the custody battle and get herself a new property. All of these scenarios were selfish. No thought or regard for the emotional impact of the kids or me. Just someone that wants what they want and will do anything to get it. Doing so and affecting Jessie's birthday is unforgivable. The timing is insane, she not only hurt me but Jessie too. The effect this will have on the kids by missing school, playing and talking with friends while also being away from loved ones will affect them hugely.

I decided to make Casey an offer which I had my 16-year-old nephew David-James deliver around 8 pm at Casey's parents home on the same day that I found out she had placed herself in a refuge for them to pass onto Casey. Stating that if the only thing she cares about is physical possessions and her goal is to have the flat, she can have it as long as she agrees to 50/50 custody of Jessie which we had previously agreed to and keeps her at the same school. These were my only terms — more than fair. I had done nothing wrong. Casey chose her actions which have negatively affected everyone around her. I was prepared to honour our original agreement before this mess and lose my home just so the kids are home, safe and back in school. I don't gain anything else and have a strong case for sole custody of my daughter, but at this moment in time felt joint custody is the fairest solution for Jessie to have a balanced life.

The next day I received a very generous surprise from my solicitors. Witnessing the dedication to my daughter and the sacrifices, I was prepared to make for her they gave me a wonderful gift. During the phone call, they informed me that there had been a meeting and a decision was made to represent me pro-bono. They won't charge me anything for their services for the entire duration of court proceedings no matter how long it lasts. All the hard work and perseverance is from the kindness of their heart. No words could come close to explaining my gratitude. My parent's had been funding my legal battle. I had been anxious about the debt incurred and the potential for bankruptcy. It wasn't their battle. It's mine, but I had no means to fund it myself. Casey had left me crippled by debt. To offer such a gift is unimaginable and unexpected. The first time in their history that they had decided to work for a client pro-bono. A huge honour, which had me in tears. To offer this for my daughter meant the world to me. They were extremely passionate about my case and the injustice. I was now only liable to pay the barrister fees for representation in court, which was a huge relief.

7

FIRST CONTACT

After four weeks of absolute ignorance, my legal advisors received a phone call from Casey's newly appointed solicitor. They explained that she had been in contact with them and they will be in contact again shortly. No further information provided. The following week they got back in touch to inform that Casey is applying for public funding for her legal challenge. To be granted funding, there must be a claim of some form of abuse. I had planned for any eventuality. Three weeks later, on June 21st, 2017, Casey's funding had been accepted, and I received a somewhat surprising and nasty letter from her solicitor. The contents were deplorable.

We understand that our client felt left with no other option to leave the Chelmsford area due to sustained domestic abuse she suffered by way of your client's actions... witnessing your clients conduct was having on our clients two daughters she resigned herself to having to remove them and her from the situation... Our client recognises that Jessie has a strong relationship with her father, but she remains fearful and concerned that this was used by your client at

times to exert control and manipulation both over Jessie and her... She believes that there is no place for your client to have a continuing relationship with Emma, on any level.

They accused me of mentally abusing Casey and Emma while using Jessie to manipulate situations. I immediately noticed that the accusations were coming from Casey's mother, but she would've had to agree and consent, which makes her just as guilty. It was made clear that there would be no further relationship with Jessie's half-sister Emma. It was a surprise as a week or two before Jessie's abduction. Casey had stated that she knows how much Emma means to me. She would allow her to stay over with me should one of us move to a new home. The allegations now are outrageous.

Having analysed her actions thus far, I was expecting the accusations against me as it was an obvious tactic to shift her severe mental health issues into her favour by making me the reason for her suffering. Very cunning though rather ungrateful. I had a difficult time reading the allegations on paper knowing that Casey would've had to sit with her solicitor and make the statement. I felt physically sick. I had always supported and encouraged Casey with everything she ever wanted. Now that she feels she no longer needs me, she's prepared to throw me away and make me suffer, no care for the consequences.

While I felt the accusations were disgusting, there was no chance of me rolling over and accepting defeat. After all these accusations are enormous. If found guilty, they could have severe consequences for me and my relationship with Jessie. I was defiant and wouldn't allow lies and deceitful behaviour to dictate the custody of my daughter. It's my opinion that Jessie deserves to be in the care of someone that truly loves her, and sole desire is not themselves.

It transpires that Casey had relocated a vast distance up north to Liverpool. A major city with high crime rates, a place she has never visited before and doesn't know anyone. Before our relationship, Casey would often move back and forth between locations every time a relationship ended. She struggles to cope with situations, running off and leaving everything behind for a fresh start with no regard for the chaos she leaves behind or those she's affecting.

The positive for me was that after two months of trying to engage in communication with Casey contact and dialogue had finally been established. Before this, there was a serious consideration to hiring a private investigator to locate them though it would've been an expensive option. I had also been advised to stake out the grandparents' home in the eventuality that Jessie visits. The solicitor's indicated that should Jessie be in the care of anyone other than the mother then I have the legal right to remove her from them and take her into my custody.

The plan was to call the police as back-up, should the situation arise to uphold my legal rights, without an altercation. I watched the grandparents' home from across the street as advised for a short period. Though felt it would be doubtful that Jessie would be in attendance, as their home is near her school.

I attended my solicitor's office to sign court application papers for Liverpool Family Court. These were filed 22nd June 2017 the day after receiving Casey's solicitor letter. The response was immediate as there had been enough delay. We wanted court proceedings to commence as soon as possible. The advice received was that applications take 7-10 days to process. A letter was also sent to her solicitors to inform them of my position.

While your client's instructions and ours appear diametrically opposed, our client is at least relieved that your client has sought your advice and that there is a source of contact between us… Our client will be making an application which will be filed at Liverpool Family Court for a Residence and Specific Issue Order… Our client was your client's carer… We are instructed that your client does have mental health issues… You can understand, therefore, that our client has very real concerns about your client's ability to cope and, in particular, the impact of your client's recent actions on his daughter.

Due to the nature of Casey's accusations, the process is unlikely to be straightforward and will require various hurdles to get through to eventually get custody proceedings established.

In the meantime, it's hoped I will be able to see Jessie in person for the first time in months while the court process is taking place. For now, a card was sent for Casey to give Jessie. If she receives the card, it would be her first contact with me since she was abruptly taken away without warning. I was sure that she would be emotional reading the short note.

I had been overcome with emotion while writing the card and reading it back to myself. Any mention of the birthday card had me overwhelmed and distraught. I was so affected that I struggled to continue discussing the case with my family and also overcome with tears during a meeting with solicitors. I wasn't free to express myself or have a natural conversation with my daughter. I felt as though I was being treated as a criminal.

For a few months before this saga, we had been left alone weekends while Casey frequented to Kent. No regard for leaving the kids behind or any effort to communicate with them while she was gone. But now she felt it's appropriate to take them away without warning and dramatically change all of their lives. Make outrageous allegations that her daughter's father is an abuser. Either forgetting or choosing to ignore all the support, love and effort I had put into everyone's lives. I was always there when. When Casey needed me to take her somewhere, I would take her. Not without debate as I was asked so often, it became exhausting. Kids have parties to attend, sleepovers, days with friends or school events. I would be there taking them and attending and recording those moments to cherish in years to come. While this situation continues, I created separate DVD's of Emma, Jessie and myself from home-video recordings and photographs. I watch them every day and often cry — so many wonderful memories.

A letter was prepared from Jessie's previous school at my request. Upon hearing from my solicitors that it's ready for collection from the school, I drove there immediately like a courier. I was collecting the document from the school to take it to my solicitor's office. We wanted it on file and submitted ready for court. I was being portrayed negatively by Casey. The teachers at the school had witnessed me drop off and collect the children from school. I was always in attendance, as reported in the letter.

The father attended parent evenings and open evenings on a regular basis. He frequently dropped Jessie to school and picked her up and always attended Jessie's class assemblies.

- School letter / July 2017

I had hoped for more information; however, my solicitors were happy with the contents. It was apparent that the school didn't want to get involved in the legal proceedings any more than necessary. At least it was a start to confirming how involved I was within Jessie's schooling.

8

ARGUMENT

The biggest blowout in our relationship occurred April 21st, 2017, just three days prior. Casey had regularly abandoned the children weekends to stay with her cousin Jack in Kent. I had become suspicious about where she was going and with whom. Relations between us had been strained for many weeks. Casey had said she visits him as "He's the only one that really knows me". It made no sense to me as I felt that having lived with her for almost eight years, no one knows her better than me. As time moved on, we had become opposites, struggling to agree on anything regardless of how trivial.

Unprovoked and entirely out of nowhere, Casey became irate swearing with incredible rage and anger just as I parked the car. The kids had been dropped off to school. We were about to collect a dog to walk. A task we did daily while the kids were in school. Shocked and confused, I had no idea where all of this was coming. She had recently returned a few days prior from frequent weekends away. It became evident that whoever she had been spending time with was either manipulating or encouraging her to argue with me to make our life together uncomfortable.

I don't like to see Casey upset, but I will always hold my own when confronted. I'm not violent but will stand up for myself. Enduring a barrage of abuse took its toll. I tried my utmost to remain calm, but the restraint reached its limit. I retorted by shouting back at her, telling her what I *really* think about these weekends away, her behaviour and my true feelings about her family members. Everything I had been holding in for so long had finally surfaced. They are great at talking the talk, but when it comes to doing anything, they are never there for her. I lost respect for them a long time ago to the point where I hadn't visited their home for a long time. I made a point of vacating the living room whenever they visited though this was very rare indeed.

Casey was fuming. More so than she was at the start. I hadn't held back in my assessment. The mood was agitated and volatile. Both were having an immense amount of hate towards one another. On this occasion, I remained in the car, doing my best to calm down and relax listening to music. Casey walked the dog around a nearby field though cut the walk short as she struggled to focus.

After returning the dog to its owner, the drive home was incredibly tense. Hardly a word was said until she started up again with more complaining and accusations. I did my best to remain calm. Her behaviour worried me immensely. I already knew that she was unpredictable and very impulsive. There was a real concern that she may do something untoward. I wasn't sure what, but she is capable of anything.

I warned her that if she ever does anything to cause Jessie to be distressed or she loses the laughter and joy in her heart that I will do everything to make sure she is in my care. It's not my intention for us to go through court, but if I must, I will do everything for her. Casey became defensive and unpredictable. She was threatening to jump out of the car while we were driving at speed along a country lane. Upon arriving home, she was enraged shouting. I demanded she get out of the vehicle and that she is never to be in my car ever again. I was fed up with being treated so horrendously when I had been doing everything to support her. The lack of respect was unforgivable.

Casey phoned her father. I could hear her saying she can't cope anymore, complaining and making me out to be a lunatic. As always, she is the innocent victim in her stories. I'd had enough listening to the conversation. I suggested she just put the phone down and we go to the council and sort out our living situation once and for all. Casey agreed though refused to leave the car upon arriving at the council offices. After some persuasion, she joined me. The advice received is that one of us had to remove our name from the joint tenancy which neither of us was prepared to do. I'm honest and would allow her to remain living at the flat until she finds a new home. She didn't like the flat anyway. I didn't trust Casey at all. I knew that she would evict me at the earliest opportunity, regardless of what she says. She can be very deceiving and selfish.

The mood between us had relaxed, and conflict temporarily receded. Casey made herself comfortable on the sofa while I made a cup of tea before retreating to the bedroom to work on the computer. The kitchen had become a source of irritation for weeks. I'd had no assistance with the chores and tidying of the home. The washing-up wasn't done for a few days. I intentionally avoided it to see if she would be pro-active and try to wash-up. I raised the issue before she got too comfortable watching a movie. She responded that she's going to watch the horror movie then do the washing-up when I leave to collect the children from school. I would've preferred it be done now to make sure it's done but chose just to accept her intentions to avoid any further arguments.

I was shocked upon arriving home with the children. It was evident that there had been no attempt to wash-up. It had been Casey's suggestion to do it when I collected the children from school so I couldn't understand why the mess remained. Confronting her just made the situation more confusing. The excuse was that she had been packing Emma's bag for a sleepover at school and now she is running a bath for Jessie as she has a birthday party to attend. By this point, I was fuming. There was no excuse. I made my feelings very clear. Emma was more than capable of packing her bag. Had the washing-up been done by the time I arrived home. I could've cooked the dinner while she tends to the bath, but now there wasn't enough time to wash up and then make the dinner. I was personally starving as we hadn't eaten all day, and the children needed a meal before they go to their respective group activity.

Casey was surprisingly calm. It was her opinion that we could stop at McDonald's on the way to the birthday party. I explained that there wouldn't be enough time as we're now behind schedule and are likely to be late. She was never very good with the logistics. Always leaving me to decide then blame me if it doesn't work out. Essentially leaving me to take on the burden of determining so she can be free from blame. As we approached the junction to McDonald's, I asked what we are doing, whether I'm driving into McDonald's or just going to the party. Casey told me to decide. I told her that the decision is hers as I'm tired of always choosing and then being blamed. Realising the apparent situation of being late for the party, she decided to go directly there without stopping. She suggested Emma can have something to eat at the cafe. We arrived to find the cafe closed. Only snacks were available. Emma wasn't happy and didn't make the situation easy for anyone. She was refusing all food suggestions. Nothing was good enough for her. I felt the situation was an absolute mess and so avoidable. If only the washing-up had been done as agreed.

I watched Casey try to make the best of a bad situation. In all honesty, I felt she was doing well with the options she's suggesting, even persuading the staff to make a sandwich. It was Emma causing the problems by consistently refusing everything offered. Eventually, she had to make do with simple snacks of chocolate and crisps. Towards the end of the party, I asked Jessie if she could get Emma some food remaining from the party table. She returned with pizza, sausage rolls and snacks. Always helpful and considerate of others.

There was more shock to come. Casey asked if there would be time to stop at KFC after the party. My response was simple though in hindsight rather sarcastic "How can there be enough time to stop when the party finishes at the same time, Emma is due to be at her sleepover? Soon as it finishes, we are already late."

Casey was surprised. I was staggered by her confusion and didn't know what she was expecting. As I said earlier, she doesn't think about the logistics or reality of what is needed to get from one place to another. At her request though we stopped at KFC on route to the school much to my reservations. It was a day from hell with no end in sight. Upon leaving the drive-thru, Jessie's box of food tipped onto the back seat which had sand from a recent school project. Casey was fuming, shouting at me in full view of the children. I had navigated the round-a-bout slightly too fast to make up for the time wasted. I suggested she calm down and that when we stop, I'll give Jessie some of my food. Jessie was excellent about the situation though Casey was like the devil possessed. As we got closer to our destination, she started giving some of her food to Jessie while looking at me with disdain. A blatant attempt to anger me. I ignored her and provided some of my food to Jessie as promised upon arriving.

Emma felt anxious when we arrived at school. Casey had made a massive scene in the car which had upset her. She had suggested that Emma won't be allowed to take food and may not even be admitted to the sleepover as we are late. Emma felt very insecure and worried. I told Casey to calm down. I then mentioned that I had already told Emma in the morning to inform the school that she will be a little late as her sister has a party to attend. Emma confirmed that they are aware of the arrangements. I suggested she doesn't worry then as everything will be fine. Casey walked her into the school with the food. Upon returning to the car, I asked if everything went fine. She replied bluntly, "yes". My response was simple, "good".

The drive home was rather tense and quiet. This was to be the calm before the storm.

As we arrived home, Jessie went to her bedroom to play. I made myself comfortable on the sofa expecting the stress of today to be behind us. Casey didn't share that same expectation. She was ready for another round of arguing, shouting at me that she is going for full custody with no consideration of whether Jessie can hear. I was shocked as we had already agreed that we would do 50/50 shared care as it is in Jessie's best interests. Jessie had already expressed a desire to reside with me rather than her mother and sister. She understood what that would entail, but it's what she wants. Our bond is incredibly close as it has been from the moment she was born. It was my suggestion after Jessie had made her feelings clear that maybe then 50/50 would be the best arrangement so she can spend time with everyone evenly. It made her very happy. Casey had then agreed, so I didn't understand the change in arrangements now.

I made it clear that if she's going for full custody then so am I, but for her to get full custody, she would have to prove I'm an unfit father. She responded, "You're a great father". She then asked about her.

I explained, "You can't wash up or cook dinner, let alone look after the kids. If you can show me that you can step up and do those then I have no problem with our original agreement."

I don't know what she was expecting me to say. Criticising her doesn't come easily for me, and I certainly don't take any pleasure from it. I would be thrilled if she were the caring, nurturing and playful parent that I am, but she isn't. Throughout my daughter's entire life, I have been the one responsible for everything. It is for this reason that our bond is so strong. We do have incredibly similar personalities, which makes everything effortless between us.

I sent a text message to my mum explaining the need to get a solicitor as Casey is mentioning custody of our daughter. Mum promptly messaged back to say that she will call me. I replied to wait. Explaining that it's not a good time as I think it will push Casey over the edge. I was worried that she would become very paranoid.

Surprisingly my phone rang. Mum was calling. By this point, she wasn't interested in how Casey is feeling. She had witnessed enough over the past few weeks — all the torment and abandoning of the kids and now this. I answered the call in the bedroom. Jessie came into the room shortly after while I was talking on the phone. She was concerned and told me, "Mummy's crying". I responded with shock, "Not again." I then explained to my mum "Casey is upset. I'll call you back".

I was walking into the living room, every intention of comforting Casey and let her know that we can resolve the situation without drama. Those good intentions waned when I witnessed her in tears on the sofa, talking on the phone. It was evident to me that she was feeling sorry for herself and more than likely making up stories to whoever she is speaking.

Three days later, my daughter would be abducted from school without warning by the mother of my child.

9

DEPRESSION

The profound sense of loss and feeling of hopelessness was overwhelming. Positive thoughts eluded me, replaced with an aura of negativity and bewilderment. The drain on my mind and body was immense. Performing simple tasks around the home had now become cumbersome. Random unscheduled naps became a regular occurrence as my mind couldn't maintain the constant flurry of thoughts working their way into my soul. Sleeping at night was difficult. My mind was in over-drive, not allowing for a much-needed respite and never allowing me to feel settled or comfortable. It was the absolute definition of depression, a severe mental illness, which affects most people during their lifetime. Some have mild symptoms, whilst others are severe.

Each day was an incredible battle to get through without feeling tormented, abuse of the most unimaginable cruelty. Throughout our relationship, I had supported Casey with all of her issues, remaining stable and comforting. In her own words; I was her rock. To now push me to the brink of my existence was pure evil.

Family and doctors were concerned about my health. It became apparent to all those around me that I was at my most vulnerable and in total despair. I had always been mentally healthy. Never allow circumstances or people to make me feel low about myself.

My daughter happened to be my weakness, the one thing that could truly break my heart. She means the world to me. The pain I endured was for her more than myself. My heart utterly is broken, but I knew hers was too. It was hopeless. There was no way to resolve the situation. More than anything, I wanted to fly in like a hero and make everything better, but I didn't even know where she was. Couldn't reach out and cuddle her or tell her that I love her.

Photos, home-videos and songs contributed to the uncontrollable release of tears flowing down my face. Even moments when I felt fine were fraught with vulnerability as I cried without warning. I became reclusive, only venturing outside when there was no alternative. Wearing sunglasses provided me with a shield to hide the tears from the outside world. The life I had built and cherished had been taken away from me in an instant, replaced with incredible loneliness and isolation — a stark contrast to the experience I had loved.

My mind in torment. Even through all the suffering, Casey had made me endure; I still loved her immensely. While the primary source of sadness was the sudden loss of my daughter from my life, there was also a lot of pain for losing Casey. For all her failings and indiscretions, I felt that we were meant for each other. I loved her more than she would ever know — something I, of course, regret. Not telling her often enough or maybe even showing regularly.

For a long time, I blamed myself. Bore the responsibility of everything that had happened. It was my fault. If only I had been more comforting, understanding and loving. All of this wouldn't have happened. Everyone would still be home. Life wouldn't have changed so dramatically.

The reality was that I did the best I could. Casey didn't show much love towards me. She was often hot and cold. It was difficult to be affectionate when the other person doesn't appear happy to be with you. There were moments when she would adore me, but then it would change so quickly. It was incredibly confusing.

I had to compose myself between all the suffering and concentrate for the periods my mind would allow to build a case for court. There were many messages to retrieve and document. I worked tirelessly and diligently to gather everything that would be useful. Record and note my thoughts to help cope with the torment. It reached the point where my solicitors had to assert control and inform me not to send any more evidence unless requested as I had inundated them with too much paperwork — an entire drawer filled with my case files.

Remembering how Casey had dealt with her depression, I decided to try exercise. A great source of self-healing. It broke up the days to make them seem shorter and more manageable. The activity made me more tired than usual, which helped with sleep. The main benefit though was that I was beginning to feel better about myself.

Another source of enjoyment and distraction was singing along to the music, recording the moments in the car and at home to share with the world. The videos gained more likes than I had expected, which was a bonus.

Time is a healer though each day felt like a week. A month felt like a year. My daughter was a lifetime away. I had to get myself healthy and back to the person I was before all of this happened. My daughter needed me to be at my best to fight for her. I slowly began to regain my mind from the evil that had conjured a spell of destruction upon it. Strength returned, and spirit restored. Not without relapses in-between, the ensuing battle was long and demoralising.

10

FIRST COURT HEARING

The response to my court application was swift with a hearing date set for the 4th July 2017 in Liverpool. I was relieved to finally be at a stage where decisions are made by people more responsible than my daughters' mother. Had she remained in charge of the decision process, it is clear that she would never have permitted contact with my daughter again. For no other reason than her jealousy of the fact that my daughter adores me, and we have a deep connection. It was also evident that she took solace from knowing that I am suffering — a narcissistic and vengeful individual.

My sister Shelly accompanied me on the long journey up north to Liverpool. A city I had never visited. It was to be the longest car journey I had ever driven. I would rather not have to contend with such a trip; however, the hearing had to be where my daughter is currently residing.

A hotel had been booked just outside of the city. On the map, it appeared to be a rather short journey to the court building in the morning. Traffic though was shocking. Gridlock everywhere. All the roads leading in and out of Liverpool were congested and difficult to navigate quickly.

There was a concern of arriving late, but it's out of my control. I'm at the mercy of the traffic.

The stressful drive reached its conclusion with a fortunate on-time arrival. Alarms reacted to my belt as I walked through security — a regular occurrence upon each entry. Reception staff advised me to sign in on the 7th floor. There was confusion when arriving via the elevator. A sign-in desk was missing.

I decided to wait in the chairs provided for my appointed barrister. After waiting for more than fifteen minutes, a court clerk advised that the hearing is now on the 5th floor. I wasn't impressed with the changes considering I had been instructed to be on this floor. Booking in on the 5th floor was simple. A clerk was available at the desk immediately opposite from the elevator. Providing my name allowed me to be booked in for the court hearing.

My appointed barrister Miss Choi greeted me with a polite and calm demeanour. I didn't expect to have to recite everything that had happened; however, she wanted to hear the background and case from me. She had read the notes provided by my solicitors but wanted an honest assessment from me. Emotions consumed me while explaining my predicament. All of the memories and suffering came flooding through without warning. I didn't expect to be crying in front of a stranger I had only just met. Like my solicitors, Miss Choi could see that I was sincere and honest. My only focus was my daughter.

I had arrived expecting her to be returned to my care immediately. In my mind, she had been relocated without my agreement. By law, I have equal rights as Casey. She broke the law by removing her from my care and relocating without consent. I didn't realise the first hearing is a preliminary hearing with limited powers to intervene. I was in shock. It wasn't what I travelled so far to witness. Jessie was supposed to be coming home with me today.

Miss Choi advised the procedure and what to expect from today's hearing. She explained that there would be many hearings and the process to conclude will take a long time, which will be very expensive. I was incredibly disappointed and struggled to process what is happening. None of it made any sense to me. While I was upset, Casey's solicitor came into the room to speak with Miss Choi and present an offer to us. Casey would consider my contact with Jessie though there were no guarantees. In return, she wanted me to abdicate my legal responsibility for Jessie. In essence, give Casey the sole rights to Jessie's welfare. I would lose my rights to bring her home on a 'maybe'. The situation was ludicrous and nothing like what I had expected.

I was shocked by the audacity. Miss Choi advised me what is being offered and strongly recommended that we don't accept the offer. Especially with there being no guarantees. The loss of parental responsibility wasn't to be permanent, but it is a step towards making it easy for Casey to gain custody. I declined immediately. I hadn't come this far to provide her with everything on the first say so. My intention is the swift return of Jessie, not have her reside up north.

The court hearing ended with the deputy district judge requesting an urgent hearing on the next available date. A provisional hearing date of the 28th August 2017 was allocated as a back-up to ensure a date is available. In the meantime, Casey is to pass on letters I send on a fortnightly basis to Jessie. She is also to encourage and help Jessie reply with messages of her own. I am permitted to send small gifts such as magazines.

Casey had demanded any physical contact with Jessie to take place in a supervised contact centre. I was absolutely against this notion. It made no sense considering she was with me all the time before her abduction. Casey had no problem leaving her with me when she absconded weekends. The option though remained a possibility. At the very least there's a chance to see her in person before the next court hearing.

11

SUMMER 2017

The summer holidays were usually the happiest moments of the year for the children and I growing up. We would visit my parents' home and have fun in the garden. Paddling pools and tents were erected and used for hours of enjoyment. Water hoses sprayed during water fights leaving everyone drenched in fits of laughter. Watching the kids at their happiest and being a part of those moments will remain with me forever. It's easy to take something so simple for granted. When it's gone, it is a large part of life removed. Often the most simple and basic things are what give the most joy. I embraced all the good times with the kids. Always ready to be aloof and have fun. I'm a big kid at heart, so I join in with all the immature and silly games. Casey would tend to sit and watch rather than participate. It's not only sad for me that we can no longer have those moments together. I'm sure the children are unhappy too. It should never have had to come to this.

Just a couple of months before the abduction Casey suggested were we to separate she would like us to go for a meal together with the kids as a family once a month. At that time, she was thinking of the children, and as she had said previously "Regardless of what happens we are best friends". Our chemistry together is positive, and we get on so well when we're not arguing. Something changed during her weekends away. It's just incredibly sad that the events that unfolded and the decision she made affected everyone from the kids to all the extended family. Both sides of the family reside near me. There's no logical reason to explain such a drastic change.

This year was much lonelier for me with no contact permitted. I was at Casey's mercy. Not a good position to be in at all. It was rather cruel on Jessie too. Emma had spoken to her father on the telephone and was due to spend some of the holidays in our hometown of Chelmsford with her father and grandparents. Throughout the years, they haven't had a close or affectionate relationship. He wasn't reliable and hardly showed any regular interest in his daughter. Emma was only interested in seeing him when she was bored or wanted something. Other than that, she just wasn't interested.

Jessie and I had a fantastic relationship which should be embraced, not restricted. We were inseparable and incredibly close, yet for now, our contact reduced to a letter. She can't come and visit and see all the family she had been forced to abandon. There was no justice in the world. I knew she was suffering and heartbroken. While I couldn't see or speak with her, I could feel it inside of me. I could sense the pain within her. The thought of her witnessing her sister speaking with her father and not being able to do the same with me is incredibly heartbreaking. To also know that she is going to be spending time with her father near me must hurt a lot too. As her parent, I would never put her through such an ordeal. The issues I have with the parties involved don't extend to her relationship with them.

I freely admit that it's my opinion that I am a better parent for my daughter. For her entire life, I had been her primary carer. The responsibility of doing everything always fell onto me, which I embraced and accepted. My daughter comes first in everything I do. There's no hidden agenda or using her to hurt the other. She comes first, period. The same doesn't hold true for her mother. It's evident more than ever that the top priority is herself, not the children.

I had been writing and sending letters frequently, in accordance with the recent court order. Sitting down and writing each letter bought to the surface all the love and emotions. Each letter had me in tears as soon as the pen touched the paper. It was genuinely heartbreaking having to reach out and speak to my beautiful child through a simple piece of paper.

After sending a few letters with not a single reply, my solicitors sent a letter enquiring to Casey's legal representatives. The response was shocking and manufactured — more evidence of the lies coming from her.

Please note that our client simply indicated that it was an agreement that she would encourage Jessie to respond as opposed to force her to do so. We have spoken to our client today, and she has indicated that

they have had quite a busy week due to the fact that it is the last week in school.

The suggestion is that Jessie doesn't want to communicate, and Casey had been too busy with school runs to sit down with her to help do a letter. It was absurd. Jessie never wanted to leave our home, let alone be forced to relocate such a vast distance away from her family. She absolutely would want to speak to me. The other point of not having time was ludicrous. A letter doesn't take long to write, and even if the school was an issue, there's always the weekend.

Letters were proving to be more difficult than expected. Attempts were then made to try and commence supervised contact. While there shouldn't even be any suggestion of it being required, I wasn't in a position to argue it without waiting months to get to that stage in proceedings. Any chance to spend time with Jessie is worth it whether the circumstances are justified or not. As we move forward, there is a process to adhere to, claiming unfairness won't get anywhere. I have to take each stage at a time. The first hearing provided an opportunity for contact under specific conditions and letters up to the next court hearing. Those are the only options available unless Casey miraculously changes her stance, which would be unthinkable because of her actions thus far. Hopefully, soon, the contact options will expand into something of a relationship between Jessie and me.

At my request, the contact centre's information was sent from Casey's solicitors. An application form needs to be submitted. First, my details are to be added and then Casey's. I had to initiate so that I don't see her information after. I'm not permitted to know where she is currently residing. A ridiculous situation due to her claiming abuse. She must be protected for now while her lies are not tested. Makes no difference to me as I have no interest in her, aside from our daughter's welfare. Playing the victim doesn't bother me in the slightest. She's the one that has to look herself in the mirror one day and be proud of her actions. I can't say that I'd be too proud of myself if I had treated her and our daughter in the way she has throughout this saga. But then again, we have different mentalities and morals. It is usual for her, so she may never grasp the gravity of her actions.

12

CANCER

A hidden evil that lingers and slowly spreads throughout the human body. An unforgiving and uncompromising disease that doesn't discriminate between young or old, male or female, race or religion, rich or poor. There are no exceptions. No-one is safe.

There is only one word that strikes more fear into the human soul than 'shark' or 'fire'. That word is CANCER. Everyone suffers, from the host to their loved ones. It is cruel and relentless.

In 2013 my stepdad was diagnosed with cancer. As is the case with all diagnoses, it was wholly unexpected and shocked the entire family. Everyone handles trauma differently. I try to keep my feelings inside until I'm alone. Only then do I process my thoughts. I don't think it's fair to put the burden of one's grief upon the person that is still processing their mortality. Of course, it's not as simple as that. Once the tears begin to surface, it's incredibly hard to stop the process, as my sister could testify.

I hugged him. Told him the love I have and how much he means to me. A strong man, head of the household. Always the rock in the family. Even while everyone was processing everything that is happening, it was him that was comforting others — placing their needs above his own. He typified everything great about humanity.

It wasn't the end, just the beginning of a long and exhausting battle against the hidden enemy. Some drugs and treatment worked while others didn't. There were good days and bad. The bad days were torturous for him though he tried not to show it. He was often keeping the suffering to himself. My mum was only finding out when it became too painful. She would be critical and explain that he needs to inform her whenever there's a problem. It just wasn't in him to be anything other than the strong pillar of the family. He never liked to burden anyone or ask for help.

A few weeks before the abduction he was adamant that I need to deal with Casey through Court. He had been through a similar situation himself a long time ago before his relationship with my mum. The court awarded full custody of the boys. All the signs were evident to him that she can't be trusted. He felt I was incredibly naive to expect Casey to put the children first and remain co-operative regarding our existing agreement. It was my poor judgement. Holding her in higher regard, expecting the same trust and honesty as I. This was my downfall and he was right. By the time I decided to act, she had gone. If only I had taken his advice when I had the chance. That is my regret.

My daughters 7th birthday arrived while she was gone. No clue or idea where she was. How she's feeling, though I'm sure she was missing home. There was no possibility of me being able to say happy birthday as Casey had blocked all my phone numbers. It's unlikely that my stepdad would've been blocked yet. He was eager to speak with Jessie to wish her a happy birthday. There was no answer to his call and soon no more dial tone. It was clear that his phone number was now blocked along with everyone else's. It hurt him as much as it did me.

I had never missed any of her birthdays, and neither had my family. It was insulting and disgusting to treat him with such disdain. He hadn't done anything wrong and shouldn't have been victimized. Parents can argue and have differences, but it's not appropriate to make the family suffer too. There was nothing to lose in allowing a phone call.

My parents' home was open to all of us for nine months, whilst we had nowhere else to live. My mum had provided Casey with clothes and everything she needed. My stepdad was supportive and cooked meals. The thank you for that was to abandon everyone and forcibly remove my daughter from their lives just over one year later. I was disgusted. She knew of his health issues and that his time on this planet was limited. It was crucial that he be able to spend time with the children while he is healthy enough. Casey denied him the opportunity before his quality of life deteriorates.

Just a few months later in August 2017, all treatment was stopped. The battle against cancer was coming to a premature end. The focus now concentrated on keeping him comfortable as opposed to prevention. Time was now running out to get my daughter home so he can see her before it's too late.

13

DISRUPTION

I was staggered by the referral email. For Pro-Contact to take place, the costs are extortionate. It was evident that Casey is doing everything to drain all the resources from my legal fund. She also doesn't want our daughter missing home. Spending any amount of time together will bring all those familiar and loving memories back to her.

We can offer supervised contact at our centre, but a referral would need to be made… We charge a non-refundable £50 referral and administration fee and £100 for a two-hour contact session. If written recordings are required, please add another £100 per session. Sessions are fully supervised; the visiting parent would not be left alone with the child at any time and would not be able to take her out of the centre.

Of course, to make it as expensive as possible, Casey wanted everything the centre had to offer. It beggar's belief that contact will cost £250 at a time plus the additional costs of £100 in fuel and food. A £350 total fortnightly cost on top of court proceedings. Money that could be spent on giving Jessie a good time, having a fun day out. Her selfishness has no bounds. I regularly think of her as a narcissist as she never does anything to dispel that thought from my mind. No good comes from her just deception, selfishness and pure evil — a role-model of the worst kind.

One would think having agreed to the contact centre. Signing the application and agreeing to pay the ridiculous fees that contact would soon be happening. In a normal situation which would be straightforward then that would be a fair assumption. However, this was a rather complicated and testing situation. My solicitors are very experienced with family court proceedings, and even they were surprised and amazed at the delays and behaviour of Casey. I did warn everyone from the start that between Casey and her mother they will cause mayhem and won't be sincere or put Jessie first in any of their decisions. Even this early on in dialogue between us, I was being proved correct in my assessment.

Weeks after I signed the application, it still hadn't been approved by Casey or forwarded to Pro-Contact. Without a completed form, they couldn't start the process of establishing contact at their centre. At this stage, I had done everything I can. Sent letters with a magazine for Jessie fortnightly without fail and signed the application for the contact centre. In stark contrast, Casey wasn't providing Jessie with an opportunity to write letters in response and delaying any possibility of contact. It was abundantly clear that this is going to be a brutal battle to overcome fully. The only hope of getting anything positive is to force her hand through the courts. She isn't going to do anything right by her own free will.

The weeks passed without any confirmation of the next court date. At the recent hearing, the judge ordered the next available date after 28th July 2017. That date had been and gone with no further communications from the court. Frustrated and exhausted by Casey's behaviour, I harassed my legal representatives regarding the next court date. They were equally frustrated and perplexed by the family court system in Liverpool. By all accounts, the Chelmsford courts are more efficient and responsive. Liverpool family court was proving to be the opposite. No-one seemed to have any answerers to requests for clarification. The buck passed between pillar and post, from one person to the next. Meanwhile, my daughter stuck in the middle of this mess. She deserves so much better from the UK legal system.

A response was finally received. The situation was worse than expected. The provisional date of 28th August 2017 vacated. Now I was at the mercy of the court to find a new court date soon. There's a risk that the next court hearing will be after the original date. It was shocking. Why on earth would it be retracted without a new time confirmed? The court appeared to be in meltdown — utter disarray. My faith in the family court was waning as quick as it started.

Receiving a phone call from CAFCASS officer Sarah couldn't have come at a better time. They are responsible for safeguarding a child's welfare during court proceedings. Their role solely focused on the children, perfect for me as our priorities align perfectly. Everything I do is for Jessie.

Upon explaining the situation from the very start to the current predicament, she was shocked. I had taken up an hour of her time making sure to leave no stone unturned. Sarah was adamant that if what I had said is true than Casey has committed perjury. She was my saviour in a moment from hell, taking it upon herself to contact judges in the family court to request an urgent hearing. Astonishingly a court hearing scheduled within a week. A fantastic effort from at least someone that seems to have the best interests of Jessie as their top priority. After so much frustration and numerous failures within the system, hope was shining through.

Miraculously just after the phone call with Sarah the contact centre application was sent by Casey. Much to my surprise, I received a phone call from Pro-contact while I was at the gym. I didn't feel the need to continue with their services with the court hearing just a week away. It was about a month too late.

As there was no guarantee that the upcoming hearing will go in my favour, it occurred to me that it may be useful to start the process to prevent any further delays. Just as a back-up option. Upon enquiring of the stages required to get their services commenced, it became clear that it wouldn't be worth starting until the court hearing had finished. An upfront fee was needed. Then Casey and I would need to attend separately to be interviewed before a visit with Jessie can be booked. That would require a very long journey for myself to have a conversation with someone in person. Even then, that would be at least another month. I explained my upcoming hearing and felt it would be sensible to await the outcome before progressing with their services any further. With Sarah getting an immediate court hearing, it was very likely that contact would be commencing without the need for any supervision. She was confused as to why it was requested in the first place. There was nothing to suggest that Jessie would be at risk of any harm while in my care.

14

CASEY

Nothing made sense anymore. My mind was torn and confused. One moment I hated Casey for all the pain and suffering Jessie, and I had to endure. The next I was missing her profoundly. Our life together meant the world to me. I was often blaming those around Casey for manipulating and guiding her negatively. It couldn't be her fault. She wouldn't do this willingly. I couldn't fathom at all that Casey would've decided those actions herself.

She has been challenging and disruptive though it's essential for me to take a step back and rekindle those positive feelings and memories we once shared. I often try to remember the good times we had together so that I don't lose focus of what she meant to me. After all, this is the person that I felt I would one day marry. She can't be that bad if I loved her so dearly.

When the reality of the situation kicked in, there was an overwhelming feeling of hate. Especially when I thought about Jessie and the torment of separation she was enduring. The audacity was astonishing. How on earth Casey felt her actions were justifiable beggars' belief. Currently, she's very selfish with not an ounce of compassion, which doesn't help. I want to forgive and move forward, but she makes it very hard. Sadly, hate consumes us both at this moment in time. While this continues, neither of us will be able to find happiness.

The puzzle though is that she hasn't always been this way. I firmly believe that someone or a group of people have been a negative influence to manipulate her behaviour. She never takes responsibility for her actions, so all someone had to do was make her feel a victim in some way and boom off she goes. She sees what she wants to see rather than open her eyes to what is going on around her. I don't try to portray myself as perfect. If it's appeared that way, then that was never my intention. The problem is that Casey has been so negative that in comparison, my eagerness to resolve the situation and find a positive outcome makes me appear a saint.

To help work through my conflicting emotions, I made a few letters and notes. I was advised by my legal representatives not to send them, so I kept the letters to myself. They helped me come to terms with what happened and understand where our relationship struggled.

More emotions came to the surface as I had to gather evidence for court due to Casey not talking or making any attempt to resolve our situation. A very tormenting moment in my life. I had every reason to hate her. She deserved no less, but I struggled to relinquish the profound love I had. It became clear that no matter how hard I tried it was always a losing battle.

She dreams of the perfect life but doesn't have an actual image in her mind of what that would entail. Nothing will ever be good enough for her as there will always be something missing. It's rather tragic. Our life together wasn't too bad at all and was worth salvaging. I know deep down she loved me as much as I did her.

I had put my life on hold to try and make hers the best it could. When our relationship started, she struggled to cope with her life. There was no feeling of accomplishment or ambition. She didn't have any hobbies or interests. She was drinking when Emma was away with her dad. That was the extent of her life. Casey was rock bottom in a state of despair. During our relationship, I helped encourage Casey to figure out what she truly enjoys and what she wants in life. It became clear that animals gave her a sense of joy and pride. She liked to help them, and they provided unconditional love something she often struggled with from her own family.

My career and job prospects were on hold while I focused on helping Casey live her dreams. For now, the focus was Casey. Then I can get back to focusing on myself. I already had a variety of skills across a wide range of sectors along with plenty of hobbies.

In 2014 we supported local dog rescues. Fostering dogs in our own home and helping to find permanent homes for more than thirty dogs. Most coming from either poor living conditions or beaten. Each was exhibiting their unique behavioural traits from whatever negative situation they had fled. Casey would also create posters for social media campaigns. I would help and advise when needed and always be available to collect and deliver the animals along with vet appointments. We were a good team.

We had adopted a Staffie Cross from a local fosterer of the RSPCA. Witnessing their efforts for animals made us want to help too. Casey is obsessed with all animals, particularly dogs and rabbits. We don't share the same methods of training. There's a new fashion of crating a dog to calm them and promote positive behaviour. However, I prefer them to be free to roam as they were when I was a child. Casey, in charge, gave her a sense of accomplishment, so I left the training and behavioural issues to her. We didn't always agree; however, she would make the final decision.

Typically, people that have a fondness for animals and a deep connection to care for them aren't nasty people. They are usually some of the nicest, warmest and most compassionate. Casey's compassion seems specific only to animals. She, however, struggles to limit the animals in her life. Never content, always wanting more and more.

Eventually, we expanded to walking dogs while the children were at school. We were travelling throughout local locations in fields, woodlands, parks and the beach in all weather conditions. Casey enjoyed this more than me, though I did it for her. Over time I became more and more frustrated. I craved a career of my own but was always needed to drive her everywhere and take the kids to and from school. Casey also had random days of low mood when she needed support. It was impossible for me to commit to applying for jobs of my own let alone be hired. I was happy for her that she had found something she enjoys but felt trapped.

Maybe she picked up on those vibes and felt frustrated herself, or she possibly became over-confident and dismissing all of my sacrifice and efforts. There's no way to know for sure; only she knows the reasons for her actions. Either way, there was no need to do what she did. I have never hurt her. It certainly didn't need to come to this. I'm sure she will have regrets one day. I know I do. We had a better life than she appreciated at the time.

She isn't so much a people person. Shy and reclusive, only comfortable with people and surroundings which are familiar. She has personal issues to overcome from mental health to her family. I think deep down she means well but gets herself into situations which can spiral out of control. I found her vulnerability endearing. I just wanted her to be happy. Sadly, she is easily manipulated. We had a problem from 2014 for two years whereby someone was a disruption in our life. Causing Casey to feel insecure about herself and portray me in an unfavourable view. It was difficult for her to endure, and she only told me small fragments of what happened. I always comforted her and forgave for any indiscretions. She battled her demons. Didn't need me piling on too.

It's a joy to be around her when she's happy and content with life. Moments, though fleeting and rather rare are specs of life worth cherishing. My world came alive when she was smiling. For all my efforts, I couldn't maintain the happiness in her life. Nothing was ever simple, and I often struggled to understand why there was such sadness. We had a fantastic family. Children who adored us as we did them. Many pets, including dogs we had adopted. Life was good. I'll never understand.

From her perspective, there must be reasons. As with all break-ups, there's *his* view, *her* view and the truth is somewhere in-between. I can only portray my feelings and thoughts on everything that is happening and has happened. I can't speak on her behalf for what she felt. Maybe her views contradict mine. We all see things differently. The past, however, is confined permanently to history. There is no point continuing to obsess about it. The present and future are all that matter now.

Casey is the mother of my child, so regardless of my personal views or feelings, I will always be respectful and mindful of that fact. I fell in love with her a few years before our relationship even began. We had met at local cash & carry. It was my first day upon returning for a second stint after leaving a warehouse job further away. We were introduced to work together. I was rather rude and ignorant, as I didn't want to be there. It wasn't personal, only a consequence of my mood, and lack of enthusiasm towards the surroundings. It was a step back in my career from the job I had previously worked — fewer hours, less money and very basic in comparison. The next day I was much kinder, and I would eventually become obsessed with her. I was always coming up with reasons to be near and taking something inconsequential as an excuse. We got on well, and our friendship was blossoming.

There were a few occasions whereby I would fight for her with management. Often, they would demand she does physically demanding tasks such as sustained heavy lifting. I would overrule their authority and tell her not to worry as I'll do it. There was another time when a manager also witnessed us talking and laughing while replenishing stock. He decided to make an example of us by splitting us up and giving us both a warning. It was the last straw for me. I finally snapped. Casey didn't want me to react. She was worried about the consequences. I'd had enough, though. Other people were visibly talking together while working. I stormed after the manager and confronted him. Made it clear that I'm not putting up with being singled out when other people are doing the same thing. Suffice to say he allowed us to continue working together. Deep down, I don't think I would've handled it easily to be separated. So, I fought for us and won.

One of the last interventions I did before being accepted for a prestigious job at the port of Tilbury was to stand up for Casey once more and be the voice she so desperately needed. She had been ill at work and trying her best to get on with the job though she couldn't be productive as she was struggling. Casey needed to be at home recuperating though was too afraid to speak to management herself about her health. I told her that I would take care of it. I went into their office and rather than asking, I told them I'm taking Casey home and that I'll come straight back after. I provided no opportunity for debate. What I said 'is' happening and did happen. I dropped her off outside her flat. At that moment, I was her saviour.

During our relationship years later, I would continue fighting for her whenever she needed me. For me, she was always worth the fight. I would even go and collect her from wherever she was in an instant. Whether it be a train station, open field or a vulnerable night out drinking. It could be anytime, midnight or early morning. I would be there without fail.

The full extent of my support will remain with me, not on paper. Some things are just too personal to share. Sadly now, I'm nothing more than an annoyance trying to maintain a relationship with my daughter, preventing Casey from being free to do as and what she wants with no consequences. I was fighting her for the first time in our lives because I had to. Jessie needed me to. Throughout our relationship, I was protecting and supporting her. To do the opposite and fight Casey didn't come easy. It went against everything I had done before and one of the hardest things I have ever had to do. It was either fight or disappear from Jessie's life forever. There was no other choice. I had to fight.

15

SECOND COURT HEARING

It wouldn't be unexpected to be somewhat nervous at the prospect of attending court. It's not something most people would be eager to participate in, but, for me, it was a blessing — a huge relief. The past eight weeks had been a living hell. Dealing with a crazy person doesn't do any wonders for my mental wellbeing. There were moments when I felt like I was losing the plot — questioning my sanity and whether I was over-reacting to circumstances. I wasn't sure if my anxiety of being apart from Jessie was the issue. My lack of patience and irritability. The desire for immediate results. It didn't take long for me to realise that it wasn't me at all. The problem was her. She was the one not behaving like a responsible parent.

The journey north is horrendous. The miles go on and on. Roads feel endless. While the scenery changes, it often feels the same. When there's heavy traffic, it has a catastrophic impact on the human psyche. Covering such a vast distance increases the probability of there being incidents to encounter along the way. The sat-nav estimated arrival time only considers the current circumstances. Everything can change at any moment, and it often does. A five-hour drive isn't something to savour and not without suffering.

On this occasion, I had done my research before booking a hotel. Fortunate to find one with an adjacent car park within walking distance to the court building. Significantly reducing any stress in the morning and alleviating any need to suffer traffic into the city. I was free to relax. Enjoy a buffet breakfast at the hotel and then attend with a brisk walk into court.

I shared a laugh with the waiter the night before. I can be silly and goofy, never one to conform to convention and tradition. Typically, I tend to respond in ways that most people don't. The waiter asked me a simple question, "Would you like a drink?". Undoubtedly not too complicated to answer. My response was "Yes, please." My sister Shelly was in hysterics. I looked at her as though she was the crazy one out of the two of us. "- and." Shelly enquired with sarcasm. I was completely lost. I had answered the question accurately. "Yes, I would like a drink, please." I think it's always important to have manners. Shelly followed up "What drink would you like?" Looking amazed at my level of stupidity. I was laughing after realising how fundamental my initial response was in hindsight. The waiter is very patient and amused by our whimsical southern behaviour. "Oh. I'll have a- hmmm- pe- nope, yeah OK I'll have a Pepsi please." I can never make up my mind. I'm not awkward on purpose; I tend to choose something and then wish I had chosen differently. Trying to reduce this by taking slightly longer makes me appear out of place with society.

I received a phone call while waiting outside the courtroom with my sister Shelly. It was my solicitor explaining that Casey won't be attending court today. I immediately responded "Typical; it doesn't surprise me. She won't want to face up to what she's done."

There was more to come. Jessie had trapped her hand in a fire door at the refuge, which requires surgery in hospital. I was shocked, not expecting this today. She's never been at harm in the seven years of her life with me. Now in just a few short months of being in her mother's care, she's to have surgery.

I was waiting for a different barrister today. This hearing was short notice, which unfortunately conflicted with my previous barristers' availability. I was now waiting for an experienced Mrs Flemming. Her court record displayed seniority and experience within family court amongst other proceedings. The worry I had was that I would have to recite everything that has happened all over again from the start just as I had done with Miss Choi.

An older lady had just signed in with the court clerks. I couldn't recognise her from the photo I had seen the previous day. My sister was adamant that it's the barrister we were expecting. Noticing our strange curiosity of her, she approached us and said, "Judging by the way you're looking at me, I guess you're waiting for me."

This had us all laughing; an excellent ice-breaker. Mrs Flemming seemed relaxed and comfortable to engage in conversation. There was no need for me to go into all the previous details as she had all the information she needed along with prepared notes. Being experienced, she could already see through the nonsense Casey had been putting me through. Had there been any abuse it would've been blatantly obvious. A criminal record, police report, school report; citing issues with the children, local authority. The list goes on and on, but there was absolutely no record from anyone of anything — just a fantasy story from Casey.

The incident with Jessie in the hospital was fresh. I told Mrs. Flemming about Casey not attending today due to the hospital. She rolled her eyes in disbelief. There was to be a brief meeting between myself, Mrs Flemming, Casey's legal representatives and a newly appointed CAFCASS officer, Mr Henry. The meeting was emotional and challenging to endure. Casey's legal team spoke to my barrister as though I wasn't even in the room, spouting negatives about me which weren't right. Suggestions that the mother had suffered emotional abuse, which the daughters witnessed. It was frustrating and hard to remain quiet. Eventually, I did interrupt "I'm not here to do anything stupid. Taking my daughter and not returning her would only ruin my court case. I'm the one that applied to the court, and I will win and get my daughter home. You can guarantee that. I won't stop until she's home." Mrs Flemming gave me a look of approval, seeming very proud of me. CAFCASS officer Mr Henry was equally approving of my response. Casey's legal representatives were left in no doubt of my determination and commitment to see this process through to the very end.

Mrs Flemming then put Casey's people on the back-foot. Asking what evidence, she intends to rely upon. It became clear that Casey was only relying on the testimony of her eleven-year-old daughter Emma. I wasn't surprised as all along from the very start I told my legal team she wouldn't have anything as I have done nothing wrong. I had already known that Casey and her family had been manipulating Emma the weekends Casey was fleeing away. It was hardly a surprise that she was now being used as a witness to try and validate those false claims of abuse. Mrs Flemming was not swayed in the slightest. She retorted "It's hardly surprising that she would testify for her mother, but she's too young and hardly a reliable witness." I tried not to laugh as I thought the entire situation was ridiculous.

How dare they put up so many obstacles and treat me with such contempt while tiptoeing around Casey as a victim knowing full well that her case is incredibly flimsy at best. They had no idea that I had already endured many hours upon hours of evidence gathering. An entire box of print outs from a lifetime of message histories between Casey and I proved all the difficulties she endured in her mind and the love and support I always had throughout for her. Reading those messages would leave no-one in any doubt of my sincerity or innocence. It was frustrating that the court is all about procedure. Everything must be done under the current stage in proceedings. We weren't at that stage of evidence revealing yet. I was desperate to get my proof seen so that I can be done with this nonsense once and for all.

I took my seat in the courtroom, not understanding the protocol. District Judge Smith entered the room to everyone standing. Following everyone else's direction, I stood in respect too. With a simple hand motion, the entire room sat onto their seats. Judge Smith appeared confused by Casey's absence. He wasn't impressed, but upon hearing from her solicitor's explanation, the hearing continued. To my surprise, he was furious. Not with me, but with Casey. Had she been present, she would have been in for a reprimanding. In some ways, Jessie being in the hospital was a blessing for her. Her previous statement hadn't swayed him. He saw through the weaknesses in her story. Mine was truthful and from the heart. Comparing them both it was obvious who is telling the truth, especially when comparing to evidence such as safeguarding reports etc.

Sensing Judge Smiths disdain at the audacity of Casey's behaviour, her legal team tried valiantly to defend her actions by reciting her claims of abuse. The response was swift and critical. Judge Smith retorted "That seems to be most of the cases recently." Referring to the increase in claims of abuse since the rules changed regarding claiming legal aid. They then made their case for potential contact to be supervised in a contact centre in line with the wishes of the mother. CAFCASS officer Mr Henry provided his professional opinion on the matter. His position was that he did not consider that contact between the father and the child requires supervision — a damning assessment against the ludicrous demands from the mother. Judge Smith thanked Mr Henry for his opinion and then went on a transient of thought. He was explaining to everyone in the room that he is merely thinking out loud. It became clear from his thought process that he is eager for Jessie to return home with me. Judge Smith didn't like that Casey had caused such heartache and disruption in Jessie's life and could see my determination and the suffering I had endured. I was inches away from getting her home. My mind was willing him to say it.

Knowing the law better than myself, he took a step back and explained that he isn't happy, but the mother deserves a chance to be here and explain herself. The next hearing was now booked for a contested interim child's arrangement hearing on the 8th September in just one week from today. A judgement will then decide on what contact shall be granted in the meantime by the court while court proceedings remain ongoing. He made his position abundantly clear. Should the mother fail to turn up to the next hearing, it will proceed without her. The written order states either parent as the same naturally applies to me; however, there was no concern that I wouldn't appear in court. It was clear that if she fails to attend Jessie will be coming home to me. I just hoped that she fails to arrive again. As a closing remark, Judge Smith was passionate and very vocal, stating that he would love to be there for the next hearing. But he has other court hearings booked. It was evident that he was disgusted by Casey's actions in abducting Jessie.

Mrs Flemming asked the judge what the position is on the father visiting his daughter in the hospital. The judge saw no reason preventing me, citing no safeguarding concerns. I was free to visit Jessie with the permission of the court.

Outside the courtroom, I spoke with Mrs Flemming and Mr Henry. It was my suggestion that Casey could go to the canteen when I visit the hospital. That would prevent us from being in contact with one another. Both approved and were very much in favour of it. Speaking to Casey's solicitors though wasn't as straightforward. It was not their fault but Casey's. I could sense a reluctance on their part to talk to her. It was as though she had made her position clear to them regarding contact. It was my view that they don't want to either upset or make Casey irritated. I wasn't leaving without an answer.

Finally, a response, Casey declined to reveal the name of the hospital. She didn't approve of me visiting and would only provide a direct phone number to the doctor treating Jessie. I was in disbelief. I have travelled up north. She can't be too far away yet won't allow me to visit. Surely at such a traumatic moment in Jessie's life, she would want me to be there for comfort and reassurance. Casey couldn't put our daughter's needs before her own. I was disgusted as was my sister and barrister. In all honesty, I don't think her solicitors were too impressed either. They're professional and represent their client, but there is a child in the middle of all of this arguing. You'd have to be heartless not to feel some emotion when witnessing such behaviour.

Mrs Flemming explained to me in the presence of Casey's solicitor that there is nothing she can do to stop me. If I want to, I can visit every local hospital to find and see her.

More than anything I wanted to but with the situation so delicate between us I couldn't afford for Casey to spout more lies and accuse me of anything untoward. She may even try to instigate drama between us, just as the psychic had said a few months prior. Jessie witnessing us arguing wouldn't be of any benefit. It would only cause more trauma in an already emotional moment.

Phoning the doctor had me in tears. I couldn't understand the extent of Jessie's injury. Any disfigurement or harm was heartbreaking. I was inconsolable though they soon calmed me down to explain that her condition isn't permanent. Her thumb requires surgery, but it will heal fine. She currently has drips connected to her for fluids, but she is OK and responsive. This helped calm my anxiety, but I was still incredibly emotional. I had failed to protect her. This should never have happened.

16

THIRD COURT HEARING

A week went by rather quick. The past few months had been disturbing and incredibly tricky. Each day tediously slow. Now progress is finally being made with court hearings coming in quick succession. To think the last court hearing took nearly two months to arrange and now here I am a week on from the previous court hearing ready for yet another. There may be hope yet for the UK family courts though it's probably best I don't speak too soon and jinx the run of good fortune. I've already experienced the worst it has to offer. I prefer my experience now remain positive.

This is the day I had been waiting for in such a long time. It was exciting and nerve-wracking, challenging to sit still or be comfortable. Emotions all over the place, trying my best to remain composed at least on the outside. Inside my heart was racing so fast like a beating drum though there was no music just anxiety. So much hinged on this court hearing.

I'm within touching distance of being granted permission to spend time with my daughter. More than anything I've wanted to be able to tell her how much I love her and cuddle her. Basic gestures that most people take for granted. Jessie and I always said 'I love you' to one another when we were a family at home, so it's natural for us to display affection. Reaffirm to her the love I have and that she will always be in my heart. Know that daddy will always be there for her and is fighting to get her home.

I dread to think about what lies and negative stories Casey has expressed upon her. With no direct access between us, she doesn't have much choice but to believe whatever she has been told. She's bound to be affected. It's safe to say that she may be negatively influenced. Our bond is incredibly tight though, so I wasn't worried about her hating me or anything like that. I just wasn't comfortable knowing that she has suffered emotionally during all of this. She deserves so much better from everyone.

A child should feel love, not hate. Trust in her parents and family, not contempt or uncertainty. I was not only fighting for contact between us but her future. To make sure she isn't affected too profoundly by her mother's actions. Limit the damage done and move forward with hope and positivity. Lord knows there's been enough disruption and confusion in her life already.

Against my hopes and prayer's Casey was present at court. I had wished for a much more relaxed day with the slight dream of Jessie coming home. Hearing that she was in attendance, deflated my positive mood. Another day of negotiating nothing and having the judge decide our fates. With Casey negotiating is a one-way street. She tends to wait to hear my proposals and then counters with absolutely nothing. Offers the bare minimum or whatever she can get away with without giving me anything.

No words can describe the contempt I have for her behaviour though like I say 'narcissist' is the one word that often comes to mind. I'm in attendance at court for our daughter. Travel the length of the country for Jessie. Casey arrives, and her only interest is herself. Sadly, I think her real motive for being here is to maintain her benefits. Doesn't cost her anything to attend as her legal fees are publicly funded. She doesn't have to worry about any costs associated with the Court. Heaven forbid her money decreases if Jessie wasn't with her and of course she wants to beat me. Have that trophy to wave in my face... our daughter. Charming, though the person that matters most in all of this won't be too proud of her actions. It's heartbreaking to think that Jessie is stuck with this person for the foreseeable future as she is this bad in court, it beggar's belief what Jessie has to cope with at home.

With the involvement of CAFCASS officer Ms Falmer, there was mediation between Casey and me. Our respective legal representatives engaged in dialogue together with her and then relayed her views to us. There wasn't much Casey could do about preventing me direct access to Jessie. For all her demands for supervised contact, there just wasn't any justification for it. There must be underlining reasons which pose a significant risk to harm physically or emotionally to the child, and there just wasn't any.

Between us, we agreed to an initial three-hour contact tomorrow as I was already up north, so it was an excellent opportunity to get the arrangement started immediately. Next weekend will be for five hours. I wasn't satisfied at all with the three-hour limit, and Casey wasn't pleased with five hours, which is how it came to be a progression. She got her three-hour demand, and I then got my five hours. It was being justified as a way of easing contact between Jessie and me while progressively increasing our time together. Absolute nonsense to me. We don't need to reintroduce gradually. She should be coming home to live with me, let alone a pathetic three hours together. As always, I wasn't in a position to dictate terms. I had to take what I can get. It's more than I had yesterday, and that is how I had to view the situation to make some positive from today.

I had to be seated in the courtroom before Casey could enter. The first hearing she was present in the court building but acted vulnerably to hide in a secure room while the trial proceeded. The second hearing Casey wasn't in attendance. Now she had no alternative but to attend in person.

To continue the charade of maintaining her stance of being a victim of abuse, she requested a screen. It separates us in the courtroom, and we can't then look at each other. I'm sure it was for two reasons; 1. She doesn't dare to face me knowing what she has put me through. 2. Wants the court to view her as a victim and me as an abuser. Even without evidence, the view of her behind the screen can still play on someone's mind and give the thought of something ominous.

Thankfully judge Thomas wasn't swayed by the screen and didn't favour her at all. He was sincere and fair for us both. His opinion was that there had been enough animosity and that our situation had gone on for far too long. Someone needs to take this case on and see it through to the end. He won't personally be able to due to diary commitments but will make every effort to find a suitable judge that is available.

Casey and I were emotional throughout. Any mention of Jessie's name brings to the surface all of the feelings and emotions to the fore. Everything I had been suppressing while convincing myself that I'm fine. The reality was that I'm not okay. A large part of my heart had been missing for a long time. The days, weeks and months were miserable and felt hopeless. My beautiful child removed from my life. How could I have been okay?

The only thing I can compare the situation to is losing a family in an accident. It happens so quickly and unexpected. Everyone went in an instant. No-one fully recovers from such an incident. It remains inside whether locked away and suppressed or visible for all to see. Either way, part of me died when my daughter went. I was a shell of the person I had been before. Vibrant, fun, goofy and eccentric. Now I was just serious, sad and broken. Sometimes the fun side of me would show in short glimpses; however, the light would burn out rather fast. People enjoyed my company and wanted to be around me, but I had become withdrawn. Only able to be around people in short bursts.

It was clear that Casey was feeling sorry for herself. She realises that she is no longer in control of the situation. For too long she's dictated everything. All options have gone through her. If Casey didn't want something, then it doesn't happen. Now there is a judge in charge, and that scares her. For the very first time, the realisation hits her like a steam train that Jessie may not remain with her. There's no guarantee just because she's the mother. Much to be considered. I'm sure she was worried that Jessie would also find out the truth of what happened as opposed to the lies. Everything could unravel, and she will have to face the consequences of her actions. It's for this very reason that I believe Casey wanted supervised contact. To suppress Jessie and me from speaking to each other openly.

The mother's solicitors requested the court to enforce an undertaking from myself that I will return Jessie after each contact session. If I fail to adhere, then I will be in contempt of court and face severe consequences from a fine to imprisonment. I wasn't there to play games or do anything silly. Any detrimental act would reduce my chances of a positive final resolution. My sole aim is to gain the residency of Jessie.

Judge Thomas read aloud a decree for me to accept. I spoke clearly "I do" in confirmation of my acceptance to sign a declaration to guarantee contact with Jessie and I. Made no difference to me as I intended to return her anyway. The irony of it all was that here I am undertaking a commitment not to abduct Jessie while we are in the situation because that is what Casey did. She is terrified that I will do the same thing as her.

The difference is that I'm not Casey. I think before I act. Calculate every possible outcome and place my daughter before me. Dragging her home against the orders of the court would be rather unwise. Then have her get comfortable at home. Only to be forced to return to Liverpool and then lose contact with me again. How would that be in her best interest? I have to do everything asked of me. Be the cooperative one, and make the best decisions. Lord knows how confusing the entire situation would get if I behaved anything like Casey. It would be absolute chaos.

Casey struggled to keep her composure, engulfed with emotions. She struggled with her mental health, so a stressful court hearing was always going to be more difficult for her than me. She does need to find a way to manage it, though if she's to be the primary carer of our daughter. I don't like to see her suffering, but there must come the point where her ability to maintain consistency and overcome her struggles has to be addressed. On this occasion, the judge was compassionately allowing her to vacate the court hearing early.

The court concluded with two contact sessions agreed though I needed to wait after court to sign a declaration. We don't have to wait long for the next hearing as it's on the 18th September 2017 in just ten days. The court would like to be updated on the progress of contact between Jessie and me so that proceedings can advance. A section 7 report has been ordered to be conducted by CAFCASS regarding the welfare of Jessie.

I walked away from court deflated. The day hadn't transpired how I expected. My daughter was so close to coming home at the previous hearing. I was a whisker away from hearing those words which would have been a godsend — a blessing. Now I have a battle on my hands. She can't return to me without a fight. Future court hearings would've been in Chelmsford had she come home. Casey would never endure the journey's I do for our daughter. I'd be surprised if she attended any court hearings at such a vast distance. As Jessie remains in Liverpool, we are bound by her location and will have to continue with the trials up north.

Shelly could only see the positives, "You get to see her tomorrow. You should be happy." were the words of inspiration she proclaimed. It knocked some sense into me and put what could've been to the back of my mind. I responded with enthusiasm "I'm seeing Jessie tomorrow. I have waited so long for this. I can't wait to see her. She'll be surprised to see me."

"Exactly," said Shelly

Immediately after court, I was fortunate to book the same hotel again. Only a short walk from where the handover will take place. Shelly and I enjoyed a lovely evening meal with a cold beverage before heading back to the room for some much-needed rest. Tomorrow's the day I've been waiting for such a long time. I get to see Jessie.

17

THREE HOUR CONTACT

Today is the most exciting day of my life, beating Christmas in every way. Even better than the day Jessie was born. As amazing as it was and will remain with me forever. We didn't know each other then. It was to be our first introduction as father and daughter. So much has happened since. She has grown and developed into such a fantastic child. I couldn't be prouder of her, and we are incredibly similar. Like two peas in a pod. A mini-me but better in every way. It's almost like, a rebirth being back together after so long apart. Though this time we do know each other. An immense amount of love exists between us. These are the best moments in life. Magical and worth all the suffering. Here and now is my happiest moment. The day of all days.

Shelly, Harvey and I walked into Liverpool city centre. The arrangement is for a third party to do the handover with Casey which on this occasion will be Shelly with Harvey accompanying her. Casey was playing the victim as though she fears me. I wasn't permitted to be within the vicinity of the handover. Instead, I had to wait on the periphery. I had managed to find a good vantage point to see everything from a distance.

Jessie came into view as she walked towards me with Shelly. She had the biggest smile on her face as she approached. Jessie had grown so much in just a short amount of time. Already more mature, it was frightening. When Shelly left me to collect Jessie, I was calm. No issues nor emotional. Upon approaching Jessie, I became overwhelmed with tears. It hit me out of nowhere. Suddenly all of the suffering, fighting and difficulty in getting to this moment had been rewarded. The person I had been so desperate to see again within touching distance. I never thought this day would come.

I had always been strong. Jessie had never seen me cry before. For just a moment she froze trying to contemplate what is happening. I picked her up off her feet and gave her the biggest cuddle. "I love you so much," I said with a heartfelt hug. The words I had been so desperate to say for so long. Amazingly Jessie was the calm one and seemed more grown up. She comforted me and said, "It's OK. I love you too."

To my surprise, she now had a northern accent. The accent was rather adorable though I wasn't happy that she had to change so much due to Casey's actions. I didn't say that to Jessie, though. She didn't need to hear negatives from me. A child should never separate from their parent. It should never have happened, but here we are finally together again. It was incredibly emotional.

After carrying Jessie for a while, I had no choice but to put her back down on the ground. Her weight was killing my arms. More substantial than I had remembered. Taller too.

My little girl was growing though something seemed off. Jessie wasn't behaving like she was before. We're usually really goofy and silly together. She was happy that was evident, but she lacked the individuality of her personality that I adored. My biggest fear throughout all of this was that Jessie would lose her spark and charisma. Become withdrawn and serious just like her mother. I was concerned that she had lost that positive energy or it's deteriorating. Shelly and I looked at each other, shrugging our shoulders and raising our eyebrows at the same. We were on the same wavelength. Both were seeing that Jessie isn't her usual vibrant self. It upset me deeply. I was seriously concerned about the emotional damage she had endured.

It didn't take too long for me to get the fun and silly Jessie to shine through. She no longer needed to suppress the quirky side of her personality. In my care, Jessie is free to be herself. We held hands with the biggest grins on our face as we headed into the shopping centre in search of somewhere to eat. Typically, Jessie chose McDonald's for lunch. As a child, I was the pickiest eater of the household — a bane of contention for my parents. Preparing my meals must've been frustrating beyond belief.

Jessie is worse than I. Like most kids; she has something of an obsession with chicken nuggets. The difference with her to most is that she is very particular about which nuggets she likes. KFC chicken is a big no, no for her. All she can eat from them is chips. Craziness I know. Pizza, burger and sausages are off the menu too. The best moments of my childhood aren't acceptable to her. Thankfully I know what she does like, but it's difficult to put them together; roast potatoes, Yorkshire puddings, pasta (no sauce), pancakes, chips, beans, plenty of vegetables, and of course chicken nuggets. There are only so many ways to present those options in a coherent meal. Today McDonald's can prepare the meal to her liking.

Jessie was glued to me. She wouldn't leave my side even for a moment. Accompanied me to order our food while Shelly tended to her son. Harvey was obsessed with Jessie. Desperate for her attention, he would try and do silly things to Shelly like cover her face with his hands. She wasn't rude to him just making the most of her father back in her life. It had been a difficult time apart for her, as it had been for me. We've both suffered. Cuddles and affection from Jessie were great. It was clear to anyone that witnessed us together how close our bond is. The separation apart hadn't done anything to diminish this bond. If anything, it just made us even closer.

After a couple of requests for Jessie to eat her food, she finally sat down in her seat. Removing her coat revealed the extent of her thumb injury. Heavily bandaged, although the thumb itself isn't visible, it was evident that she had suffered. Jessie looked at her thumb and then said curiously, "You know about my thumb." My response was equally curious "How do you know that I would know about the thumb?".

I hadn't spoken to Jessie directly since she was abducted. It was our first moments together again. The thumb incident was only a week prior. Casey must've told Jessie that I know about the thumb. My curiosity was peaked as I wondered what she had been told. I tried to visit the hospital, but Casey declined. She will never reveal that to Jessie as that looks bad on her. Jessie just gave me a look as to say you know. I had no idea how she would know but didn't pursue the conversation. She got up from her chair again to hug me.

Every minute counts, with our time so limited today. We were all feeling the pressure to make the most of every moment. I noticed a photo booth nearby, so Jessie and I had our photos captured. Two of the same set of four image photos printed. One set of pictures were colour, while the other black and white. Jessie chose colour photos, and I kept the black and white copies.

For reasons unknown, Shelly didn't want to use the escalators to leave the food court. Instead, she preferred the elevator. Harvey joined Shelly waiting for the elevator while Jessie, and I rapidly headed for the escalator. Whether Shelly was aware or not, she was in a race to the bottom. Jessie and I were winning. Any forward motion is a success compared to waiting for an elevator. Upon arriving on the floor below, there was no clear view of the elevator. I knew from the food court that it is to the left-hand side of the building. I couldn't understand why we were looking at a wall and not an elevator door. "It's not here, let's try going downstairs maybe it misses a floor," I said to Jessie.

"OK" Jessie eagerly remarked.

"Come on, Jessie we're going to lose the race," I said with haste.

"I'm coming," Jessie said with excitement.

We only ran where it was safe to do so, particularly alongside shops — not near barriers or escalators. I take the escalator's very seriously. Probably more so than most people. I don't mind walking up and down them while they're in motion, but I won't allow any running or shenanigans. I mention this now as Jessie had run up the escalator at an incredible speed when we entered the food court earlier. It scared the life out of me. Upon arriving at the top, I warned her not to do that even when she's with her mother. I need her to be safe.

As we approached the escalators, I made sure Jessie was behind me. There's a reason for everything I do. In my mind, Jessie being behind me is the safest option when we are travelling down. Travelling up, she would be in front of me. If she were to trip or fall, she would knock into me as opposed to her tumbling from a great height to the ground. I also stand slightly tilted so that I can see Jessie. If it isn't apparent yet I am incredibly protective. If we aren't holding hands, then most of the time I will have my arm around her shoulders.

This place was turning into a maze rather quickly. We're on the ground floor with no elevator visible anywhere. The image of the elevator flying through the glass roof in Charlie and the Chocolate Factory immediately appeared in my mind. If it hasn't arrived, it must have gone up and out of the roof. I was utterly baffled and defeated. Whoever designed this shopping centre needs their heads checked.

There's no logic to having an elevator that doesn't stop somewhere else.

Jessie and I decided to accept the victory we had earned. Without a doubt, we won. It's not our fault everyone that entered the elevator is now missing. Very mysterious, though. We did a lazy slow-paced lap around the shopping centre in the hope of bumping into our lost people. While wandering, Jessie whispered to me "You're not allowed near mummy, are you?" this was random and unexpected. It must have been one of many things on Jessie's mind that she had been struggling to let out and say. I provided a simple response "Mummy, and I no longer speak to each other." Jessie was fine with the answer as she appeared okay.

"Be good, don't be angry. You need to be good." Jessie said

"Be good? I am good. What do you mean?" I enquired.

"You used to be angry, shouting when we lived together. You need to be good." Jessie explained.

Jessie was trying to help me though I didn't understand why she was saying what was said. Casey must have been portraying me as a lunatic to everyone she meets for this to be on Jessie's mind.

"I used to shout as Emma never listened or did as instructed. Mummy never helped and made me do everything. I can't just be quiet and let chaos happen. I will be good though. I promise."

I felt it best to put Jessie's mind at ease to know that I am on my best behaviour rather than defend myself. There's no knowing what Casey had been saying and how often. The children may have heard a barrage of stories which over time can appear real. I had to be delicate to the situation. Jessie's mind then switched to sleepovers. She was desperate to come home.

I explained "For now we have the three hours today. Five hours next weekend. Mummy and I haven't agreed to anything after that, so we have to be patient. I'm sure we will have a sleepover soon though. I can't say for sure when."

"Mummy said you wouldn't return me after" Jessie suggested.

It concerned me as the judge at the recent court hearing had ordered both Casey and me not to speak negatively of one another. It was evident that she wasn't adhering to the order.

"I have no idea why she would say that. I will be returning you." I responded so that Jessie is in no doubt of my intentions.

"Do you still live in the flat?" Jessie asked.

"Yes, I'm still at our home," I confirmed.

Jessie looked confused by me remaining at our family home. The inference I got from her expression was that Casey had told her the opposite. Jessie had been separated from me for so many months during this saga. There's just no knowing how many lies she's been told or the severity of those lies. It's just incredible that Casey fed her so much false information. Her morals have no bounds.

"Can't we just go home?" Jessie asked

"No, we have to do this the right way. So, we can keep seeing each other." I assured her.

"Because of the law?" Jessie asked

"Yeah. Because of the law" I confirmed.

It broke my heart that we were bound by rules forcing her to be somewhere she doesn't want to be, and with the parent, she didn't choose.

As we walked past a beauty shop, Emma likes, Jessie asked whether we can get her something. I declined. It had been difficult enough throughout this saga to get to this moment with Jessie. In June it was made abundantly clear that I am to have no further part in Emma's life on any level. I had to take that seriously. From that moment on, I wasn't prepared to let anything get in the way of the relationship between Jessie and me. It's not nice leaving Emma out, but that's Casey's choice, not mine. I would've been happy for Emma to have joined Jessie and I. While the situation is as it is, I can't afford for there to be any accusations against me for court. I must forget about Emma and focus solely on Jessie. She is the only one in my life now. Emma and Casey are my past. Jessie is the present and future.

Out of nowhere, Shelly and Harvey appeared and greeted us.

"We've been looking for you everywhere," Shelly said while slightly frustrated.

"You've been looking for us? We've been up and down all over the place. Couldn't even find the elevator."

"It opens outside at the bottom," Shelly explained

"Well, that's stupid. Why on earth would it open outside? I've never seen an elevator do that before."

That solves that mystery though it's a poor design. Surely after people have eaten, it would be better to send them walking past shops and browsing than dump those potential customers outside. It's very bizarre. I'm just thankful that I hadn't been tossed out in the cold.

An hour had elapsed with two remaining. Instead of simply browsing through shops, I explained to Jessie that she could get some toys. She was adorable; the response made me want to get her everything.

Jessie spoke in sympathetically, "You don't have to waste your money."

"It's not wasting money. You are worth it." Responding with a proud smile.

The Disney Store was our first point of interest. We both enjoy looking through all the Disney products though I tend to find differing items interesting if she's happy though that's the entire reason to get anything. Doesn't matter how I feel about them. The perfect example is small toys that kids seem to go crazy for to then find them worthless such as Moshi Monsters, LOL and Littlest Pet Shop, to name a few. Of course, I'm referring only to girls' toys as aside from my many nephews I am surrounded by girls.

Moana was the Disney product of interest currently. Jessie loved the movie. I found the songs repetitive, but there was a strong female protagonist who is suitable for girls as a potential role model. I didn't want Jessie to choose something in the first shop she visits and then regrets the purchase if she finds something elsewhere. We left the shop empty handed with a few items to revisit should we not find anything else. Browsing throughout the store gave me some good ideas for Christmas presents. Part of my reasoning for avoiding the store for now.

While looking through books in WH Smith, Jessie noticed workbooks to help with Maths and English. She said, "Ooh, I need these." I was so proud that improving skills was important to her. I opened a math's workbook for us to try a couple of questions. Upon starting to read the first question, I became incredibly upset. Tears were flowing uncontrollably. It had been a very emotional day. Being with her felt like we were back at home when none of this happened.

It had begun to dawn on me that our time together will end soon. So I was already starting to feel a little sadness, but the main reason I got so upset was that I had been so eager to help with her education. She had been having trouble with her learning at school before her abduction. Casey and I had to attend a meeting at school. The teacher explained the need for Jessie to do extra curricula learning once a week. Even back then, I nearly cried. Her education means everything to me. She knows that as long as she tries her best, I don't mind how she scores. All we can do is our best.

I just felt that I had failed her. So much time had been spent helping her older sister Emma with her 11+, SATS tests and homework that Jessie hadn't been getting the same attention. During our time as a family, so much of my time was taken up by Casey and Emma that Jessie and I didn't get the chance to have the quality time we needed.

I had spoken to the local education authority and school while she was away with her mother. Gathering schoolwork missed and homework to help her with upon her return. Reading the math's book in the store just bought all of that to the surface. I had missed so much of her life in such a short space of time. She needs workbooks, which Casey hadn't been getting for her. It was just so sad, and we don't even have the time to do anything, let alone teach her at this moment in time.

"Don't be sad it's OK," Jessie said, comforting me.

"These are happy tears because I love you," I explained. "I won't cry next time. We'll get these workbooks so you can do them at home with mummy."

I also bought a couple of Diary of the Wimpy books. They were on a deal buy one get one-half price. It was logical to get two as she will only ask next time we're together. I was happy that she enjoys reading. She may not maintain that interest when she's older, but for now, I intend to embrace that desire.

As our time was coming to an end, we purchased slush puppy iced drinks and decided to sit outside on a bench. It didn't take long for the kids to have blue tongues. Harvey started to dance in the street to loud music coming from a live band. I then explained to Jessie that he does the worm and it's so funny. Without hesitation, Harvey dropped to the street floor, performing the worm dance move. Shelly, Jessie and I were laughing ever so loud. It was a funny moment and typified our family. We enjoy ourselves and don't tend to worry too much about the people around us.

Jessie was then the victim of my raspberry blowing attacks on her cheeks. She was ever so happy. I don't think she had laughed so hard in a long time. I would, in turn, be the victim of raspberries from her, which had us both laughing. A "Yuk" response just encouraged Jessie to try harder.

The reality of our situation was beginning to dawn on Jessie. She started to ask how long we have left though miss-spoke referring to me as Connor — quickly correcting herself with 'dad'. I'm sure she said it on purpose, but I couldn't understand why. There was a look of shock on her face when I explained fifteen minutes. I reassured her that I would be back next Saturday, and we'll be spending longer together. She responded with excitement.

Jessie informed me "I cuddle the teddy you got me and look at the photos you sent me" she had more on her mind "I put the posters from the magazines on my wall, and I want sleepovers."

She then turned to Shelly, "You can go on a tram if you want" This was funny as Jessie knew that Shelly was needed to return her after our contact has finished. By sending her on a tram, Jessie wouldn't be able to return.

She is very cheeky, but I couldn't encourage her. "No. She has to take you back to mummy."

We all walked to where I had met Jessie earlier. I hugged her and we both said I love you to each other. She appeared fine when she walked away with Shelly though she did look back and wave. I waved in response and blew kisses.

I was in shock when Shelly returned. It transpires that during their walk to Casey, Jessie had said some concerning comments. Shelly explained that Jessie had commented, "I can't tell daddy" Shelly asked, "Tell daddy what?"

"Where I live. I can't tell him where I live as mummy said he would come and smash the place up."

"Don't worry. Daddy doesn't need to know where you live, he just happy to see you."

It's very alarming that Casey has gone so far as to portray me as violent to the kids. If she has said it to them, then there is no doubt that everyone, she speaks to about our situation is going to be provided with the same story. Her behaviour is disgusting. Those accusations are unfounded and disgusting. At no point have I ever smashed a place up nor would I. The positive is that Jessie can look beyond the nonsense her mum tells her knowing that I am honest.

The sad fact is that throughout our time together, she was holding so much inside. It must have weighed on her mind. It's one thing to lie through the court to gain leverage, but Casey's taken it to a much lower level by messing with Jessie's emotions. I couldn't begin to understand the confusion she must be enduring. Casey couldn't care less so long as she gets what she wants.

18

FIVE HOUR CONTACT

It was a heart wrenching and emotionally draining journey home after the three-hour contact with Jessie. It meant the world to us to have that time together at long last. I hadn't stopped to think during all of this time, what it would feel like to be with her but to then be separated once again. It was tough to cope. The best part of me was many miles away, though no-one can take the memories. At least we have that to share.

The week had gone by rather quickly. Shelly lives approximately half the distance between my home and Jessie in the rural countryside of Norfolk. On this occasion, it was more practical for me to spend the week at Shelly's house with my nephews and her husband. A nice change of environment. There's always someone to talk to and enjoy a laugh. In all honesty, I needed a break from the predictable and isolating life I have at home. To fight in court though I need that solitude to prepare all the notes and statements. With my mind able to concentrate on just one thing I can be at my best. For now, there was no need to fight. I had spent time with Jessie and now just waiting a short while for our next contact.

Again, Shelly was the designated person to collect Jessie from Casey, though on this occasion Harvey remained at home. By all accounts, the transition went smoothly with polite smiles and hellos. Jessie was incredibly happy and smiling. She ran to provide me with a big hug as I came into her line of sight. There was no mistaking her excitement to see me.

"The days went fast. I went to bed early so I could see you sooner." Jessie explained, "I look at our photo's every day." She said with a big smile.

"It went fast for me too. I guess we were both excited." I said in response.

"What shall we get for food? Would be nice to eat in a restaurant rather than food courts."

Shelly and I had seen a Harvester restaurant earlier while exploring the area. At home, Jessie and I had regularly enjoyed dining out at Harvester and Toby Carvery restaurants. Going to another again even if it is many miles away will give us both some sense of being back at home.

"Fancy Harvester. You can get pancakes at the Harvester."

"Yeah, I like pancakes."

With Jessie in agreement, I held her hand as we made the short walk to the local Harvester restaurant. She was in buoyant mood and very cheeky. We were seated in a booth area which provided plenty of room around the table. Jessie embraced all of the space offered by jumping on me with no care for other diners. If anything, she found it more amusing knowing that people can see our antics. Casey is very reserved and wouldn't accept attention to her, so this was a rare opportunity for Jessie to let loose.

Shelly and I ordered a late fry-up breakfast before the meal options soon change to lunch and dinner. As no chips were currently available, Jessie was keen to select food from the breakfast bar such as cereals and pancakes. Sausages, bacon, hash-browns and eggs weren't of any interest to her. I helped her toast the pancakes and politely requested a member of staff provide chocolate sauce. There were many shenanigans between us with raspberry blowing on each other's cheeks and many immature games. I pretended to bite her cheeks. She countered by eating mine. Many laughs ensued. Other guests would occasionally look in our direction as we weren't exactly quiet. I didn't witness any negative remarks or expressions from people. They could see the innocent fun we were having and the love between us.

Five hours contact today provided time to explore and spend better quality of time together. I asked Jessie if she would like to go to the cinema and watch a movie or we could buy some cheap board games and take them back to the hotel and she could see where I've been staying. Jessie chose the hotel. She explained that she couldn't talk in the cinema. That was as good a reason as any. It was important to me, too that we could play and have fun. I just wanted to make sure that she doesn't get bored. It's not the same as being at home. We're forced to find activities to enjoy.

While walking towards the shops, I did silly and embarrassing walks. People would've thought I looked rather strange. I then asked Jessie "Do I look cool?"

"You walk like a girl," she said, amused.

Shelly extinguished her cigarette outside the shopping centre while Jessie, and I waited inside pretending to be statues. Shelly poked us both in the stomach at which point we both failed to maintain our poses. We laughed at our silly behaviour.

Reaching the end of the corridor entrance into the shopping centre was confusing. Shelly and I were at odds as to which direction The Entertainer shop is located. I felt that it's to our right while Shelly was suggesting the left. Jessie explained "I only believe my dad. Just my dad no-one else." I feel that she was making a more significant statement about the lies and behaviour of Casey and her family. Stating that she believes me as I'm honest and tell the truth.

We visited The Entertainer toy shop to buy a few board games; Operation, Bingo and Crazy Goggle Eyes and a hamster toy. Nothing too expensive. Costs were comparable to going to the cinema, so I wasn't trying to overwhelm her with gifts to demonstrate my love. She already knew that I love her. As with last week, she again didn't want me to struggle with buying items.

"You don't have to spend all your money on me," Jessie remarked.

That made me want to give her the entire shop. I love her personality. She is so generous, funny, affectionate and compassionate. Places others before herself. Remarkable for a child.

I explained, "Don't worry about money. If I want, you to have something I'll get it. It's not a problem."

As we were leaving the shop, Jessie made herself comfortable amongst a group of enormous teddy bears. She looked adorable. I captured a photo on my phone to remember this moment.

While walking to the hotel, Jessie made a few rather interesting comments. There was mention of her fearing buses as she had witnessed someone strangled. Casey's dad is visiting tomorrow. There was one comment that upset me deeply. I felt so bad for her but powerless to do anything. I was doing my best, but it's such a slow process through the court.

"You won't like it here. I don't, but I have to live here." Jessie said with sadness.

"I'm trying to get you home. Just be patient and never lose hope. It won't always be like this." I explained

"Am I seeing you next Saturday?" Jessie asked.

"I'll know on Monday."

"How will I know?"

"Mummy will know on Monday too," I explained

"Grandad's coming tomorrow. Not yours, mummies." Jessie informed.

"That's nice, but you can't tell me stuff for now. I'm not allowed to know." I retorted firmly.

I would've preferred to be more delicate and explain the situation better, but it was imperative at this stage of the court that she doesn't reveal anything restricted from my knowledge. I knew that Casey was waiting for an opportunity to twist something against me. She had resisted all contact between Jessie and I. The situation was too sensitive to risk any mistakes.

I put my arm around Jessie. We walked the rest of the way to the hotel attached.

Upon arriving at the hotel, Jessie was mesmerised. She had never been to a hotel before. It was an exciting experience for her. Shelly used the elevator to get to our room while Jessie, and I made use of the stairs. I asked why she wanted to use the stairs rather than the elevator. Her response was that its proper exercise. That was fair enough and good to witness her favouring a healthy lifestyle.

Entering the room elevated her excitement. She jumped onto the beds and enjoyed the privacy we finally had from the outside world. Our home, from home. It didn't take long for Jessie's attention to turn towards the many games we purchased. She enjoys bingo, and the opportunity to be responsible for selecting the numbers was too tempting for her. We put the ball pit section together after a little difficulty assembling. Small balls with numbers printed poured into the pot. Rotating the handle dropped one ball at a time. Shelly, Jessie and I were ready with two boards each. It provided a better chance of getting a complete BINGO set. It was to be a rather arduous experience as Jessie continually placed the balls which no-one needed back into the pot. I raised the issue with her though she found it amusing to witness me frustrated. She smiled every-time I complained yet continued with her routine.

Whenever a number appeared that Jessie needed, I would respond "That's nice for you." Sarcastically. As with most things, she would then do the same to me in return for the response I gave to her. I always find it funny when we share banter. It's great to have a kindred spirit. Someone that truly understands my personality and doesn't take anything the wrong way. I can come across arrogant or rude however most of the time it's part of the joke in my head. I take amusement in people taking exception to behaviour or comments when the reality is so different. Jessie understands everything I do as she is the same as me.

Our time together is always effortless. The games we played were hilarious and made us all look silly. The goggle game was entertaining. We all took turns looking ridiculous and drawing messy scribbles. The aim is to blur the player's eyes with filtered plastic glasses. The player has to draw objects on a pad of paper then. The other players then have to guess the drawing. It's an impossible game as most pictures are entirely unreadable. Some filters are worse than others. All of them are fun and challenging.

The mouth game was a lot of fun. Mouth guards in someone's mouth fully extend their lips, which reveals the teeth and gums. That player must then try and speak. The ensuing conversations are then rather amusing. Combining this game with the goggles elevates both games to a hilarious climax. Shelly was in hysterics even combining the mouth guard with glasses to try and remove plastic body parts in the Operation game. Jessie found it incredibly amusing.

Jessie's new hamster toy was frustrating. Batteries were required which I had purchased. The problem was that a screw secured the battery compartment of the toy. I didn't have a screwdriver or knife to try and turn the screw. Jessie and I went down to the hotel reception desk. The hotel staff were accommodating in the situation. A handyman came to open it for us. Jessie was relieved. We both thanked them for their assistance. With the toy now working Jessie placed the hamster in the accompanying ball. Upon putting it on the floor, the hamster ball randomly bashed into any object in its path. It was fun for a short burst. Jessie's attention soon turned to me.

A toilet break provided Jessie with the perfect opportunity to prank me. I went in the bathroom unaware of the impending shenanigans. It didn't take long for the light to turn off. Jessie couldn't contain her giggles. I could hear her through the door. Strangely the bathroom light was on the outside of the bathroom. There was no choice but to finish in the dark. Jessie was missing when I exited the bathroom. It wasn't difficult to know where she was. Constant giggles sounded from the far side of the bed. She was huddled down out of view, expecting me not to find her. I tried to make it appear as though I didn't know by calling her and searching in the other parts of the room. Then I crept across the bed slowly. Looked down at her and tickled. Laughter and erratic movement consumed her body. She couldn't control herself. It was a funny moment.

At the Premier Inn, there's a sizeable pillow in each room, which I have no understanding of its purpose. I playfully hit Jessie's body delicately with the pillow. She defended herself as best she could. It's a large pillow which is as large as her body. There's no real practical way to prevent an impact. As soon as I relinquished the cushion, it immediately became Jessie's weapon. She decided that it would be funnier to smack me with the pillow, reigning heavy blows to my head and body with this large pillow. After a few substantial impacts, I feigned dramatically to be hurt. Jessie immediately stopped trying to attack. She consoled me and made sure I was OK. My actions were a ploy, though. When she was vulnerable, I quickly tickled her belly, which had her in fits of laughter.

Jessie then looked at me then under the bed multiple times. It was evident that she was trying to mention the spare bed for a sleepover without saying it.

I said "I know what you want, but we can't today. I have to take you back."

My response deflated her. Jessie was eager to remain in my company and spend all the time in the world together. The orders of the court, however, bound us. She had to return to her mother.

Time had elapsed to within the final hour of our contact. Jessie hadn't eaten much at The Harvester earlier. She had a few snacks since but nothing substantial. We needed something quick and straightforward. There wasn't enough time for slow service, so we decided to eat at the same McDonalds which we had visited last week. On the way, Jessie consistently suggested that Shelly should go into various shops as they have *nice* things for her. She was trying to prevent the return to her mother. I made it clear that we need to behave and adhere to the agreement.

After ordering and providing Jessie with her chicken nugget happy meal, I was concerned that she was consuming the food too quickly. I didn't want her to have digestion problems.

"Slow down you'll get a belly ache," I suggested. "You can continue eating it with mummy if you don't finish in time."

"No, I can't."

I was confused. Surely Casey wouldn't have any problem allowing Jessie to continue eating her meal. For Jessie to feel concerned is somewhat disconcerting. I was frustrated for her and becoming irritated by the harmful behaviour Casey has exerted on Jessie's life.

Jessie was emotional when it was time for us to separate. Shelly was ready to walk her to Casey. Jessie broke down in tears and hugged me. I'd remained strong all day. Controlled my emotions well, but this outburst of tears from Jessie was incredibly hard to endure. I felt an overwhelming feeling of sadness. I want her to be happy. To witness her suffering affects me immensely. I was close to tears. I managed to remain composed.

"I love you and will see you soon."

We had a final kiss and hugged then Shelly walked Jessie to her mother. She kept looking back at me. I decided not to waive or make any gesture. She had to return to Casey. I couldn't afford to provoke or make the situation unmanageable by causing Jessie to run back to me. It wouldn't benefit anyone. I had returned on-time as agreed. We don't need any complications with the next court hearing in just two days.

Shelly returned to me after the handover looking distressed.

" She kept shouting. I still have four minutes!"

"Jessie broke down in tears screaming 'I want to live with my dad, you know I want to live with my dad.'"

"Casey told Jessie that they would talk later but reassured her that she would be getting plenty of sleepovers and visits." Shelly recollected

I immediately remembered a situation when Jessie had said something like her teachers at school in June. It was in a school report requested by the court. Jessie had expressed a desire to live with me and missed her life in Essex. Apparently, at that time, Casey had been reassuring of the situation. Her actions after were directly the opposite. Preventing Jessie from communicating with me. I was concerned that Casey is simply telling Jessie what she wants to hear to calm her down. Then betray her trust and not follow through on those positive intentions. With her parents arriving tomorrow, I'm sure they will attend court on Monday. Her mother is like a wrecking ball. I don't trust them at all.

19

FOURTH COURT HEARING

Before attending court today, I had a phone call with my solicitors. I explained what had happened at the end of Saturday's contact. The promises Casey had made regarding sleepovers. My solicitors were encouraged by her remarks though I urged caution. I explained that I have a funny feeling that I'm going to have to battle to get anything today. Her parents in attendance are likely to cause disruption. I was encouraged to remain positive.

Any hopes of anything positive today were dashed immediately. Casey's deception has no bounds. By all accounts, she had promised Jessie sleepovers and regular contact. Just two days later, here I am, hearing for the first time that I have been negative during the contact sessions and caused Jessie incredible distress. I knew it wasn't going to be a straightforward day before it even began. It never is, but this is absurd. I had been impeccable during the contact sessions. Diverting and stopping any conversations which I had been instructed to avoid. I couldn't have been more co-operative with the terms of the court order, which I was bound.

The fact that Casey wasn't even present during the time Jessie and I was together surely raising questions about the accuracy of her accusations. She never wanted any contact between Jessie and me on any level. Letters weren't forthcoming. There have been no phone calls. She didn't permit me to visit in the hospital. She was powerless to prevent the two short contact sessions, but at the first opportunity to be disruptive, she is reacting. Hardly a supportive parent or one that can fathom for just a second how destructive her actions have on our daughter.

Between us, nothing was going to be agreed outside of a judge's decision. Casey doesn't want any contact, and I won't accept anything less than an increase in the minimal contact we've had to endure. I've put up with enough of Casey's nonsense for far too long. There's a suggestion that there are two video recordings captured of Jessie distraught after our contact. To exaggerate further, I am accused of belittling and speaking negatively of Casey to Jessie. It's ludicrous. Casey has told her that I will smash the property up if I find out where they live, but I'm the one not adhering to the court order.

The frustration is beyond belief. I don't understand what Casey is trying to achieve. Separating Jessie and I is only going to cause long term issues between them. She won't trust her mother and will resent her. Is us spending time together really that terrible? I've learnt that there's no point trying to understand crazy people. You'll only end up more confused than when you started.

The proposal at present from Casey is for contact to reduce to supervised in a contact centre. We've been down this route before. It takes months to arrange and extremely expensive. I refuse to have Jessie feel as though we've done something wrong and that our interaction together feels like a prison. That's not good enough for me. It's not acceptable. Only a nasty and vengeful individual with no care on the feelings of a child would want that outside of an abusive partner. Casey knows full well that I'm not abusive and all safeguarding reports have cleared me of such.

Both parties failed to make progress in agreeing to future contact arrangements. The court hearing commenced with Casey yet again protected by a screen in the courtroom. Judge Mitchel provided a few judgmental glances in my direction. It was evident that this wasn't going to be a favourable hearing for me. He was aware of the accusations made by Casey and the detrimental impact I had on Jessie. For all, he knows I am a lunatic that is causing our daughter to suffer.

I understand that there is a procedure. I do worry though that it's lost on everyone else that there is a little girl in the middle of all of this. I'm here for her, not me, yet everyone else seems to have their own agenda. When I take a hit, she takes a hit too. I don't understand why people allow her to suffer. An order was made for Casey to have a psychological assessment. It was due to my claims of mental health issues, which, in my opinion, affect her ability to care for Jessie.

Casey's legal representatives wanted me to suffer financially so that I couldn't continue with court proceedings. My legal representatives had already informed me that they plan to drag out the court proceedings so that it becomes too expensive for me to continue. As the psychologist report was to benefit my case, they wanted me to fund the assessment. After looking through my income/expenditure details, the order was for costs to be deducted from Casey's public funding.

The judge made the valid point that based on my income; it wouldn't be in the benefit of the court to wait for a prolonged situation until I have the funds. It just wasn't practical to expect me to be able to fund it personally.

Without even having sight of the alleged video recording judge Mitchel ordered the suspension of contact. I was distraught. We had only just been back in each other's lives. Jessie was looking forward to regular contact with the potential for sleepovers. Now there's nothing yet again. I know that this was Casey's mothers doing. Her influence and decisions. Casey listens to her as she helped her through the custody battle of her eldest daughter before our relationship. The problem is that Carly is vindictive and has no compassion. She's never really cared for Jessie. Emma has always been her favourite. I can't recall any moment whereby Jessie was at her home without Emma present. On the flip side, Emma was regularly allowed to visit on her own.

There was a glimmer of hope. Judge Mitchel offered the opportunity for a contested hearing. It will add to the court costs substantially, which was negative. The positive outweighed the money, though. I will have the chance to present my case. Stand up for my daughter and speak openly in court to the judge how excellent the contact had been. My sister Shelly will be a witness too. Our testimonies match as we were there together. Telling the truth isn't difficult. All parties, including witnesses, are required to submit statements by 5th October 2017.

Carly's story of events is that she was present at the second return handover. She witnessed the terrible distress Jessie endured. Shelly has said that no-one else was present. Only Emma and Casey so she is lying. Came to court to support Casey as she was struggling with the stress of court proceedings. The intention was clearly to arrive. Stop the contact and go home having been successful. It went partially to plan for her. She hadn't expected me to contest the decision. Now she must do the lengthy travel again to be a witness in court and commit perjury by lying under oath. She won the first round I intend to win the war. I won't allow them to take anything away from me. If they didn't realise they were in a battle. They did now. We all left court having lost something.

The reality is it was completely unnecessary. Contact had been an absolute success. Had Jessie become used to the routine over time, she would've relaxed and been less emotional. We hadn't seen or spoke to each other in months. She was dramatically taken away from the life she loved. Anyone that's been through what we have would exert a lot of emotion. I was in tears during our first contact. Casey should have comforted and reassured Jessie when she was upset. Then do everything to make our circumstances sustainable and less problematic. Instead, she does the opposite.

I am in a fight now to get the court to overturn the decision and reinstate our contact before Jessie endures too much heartache.

20

PREPARATION

The mood on the journey back home south was low. I was sad and miserable. Shelly tried in vain to try and spruce up my dim attitude, but it just wasn't working.

Telling me "It's not too bad. You get to speak and show the court the truth."

"That's another month away. What use it that now. Jessie will be so upset and confused."

"Time will go by faster than you think."

"I don't think so, and she'll be struggling to understand."

"Keep your chin up. She knows your fighting for her."

"Right now, I'm losing and failing her."

"No, you're not. It's just a bump in the road. You'll get it overturned at the next hearing."

I struggled to get past the current situation to see the big picture. Shelly was right. If I focus and use the time, I have to prepare; then I will get this decision overturned. They're the ones lying and will have to keep up that lie while keeping their stories in sync. Shelly and I will tell the truth. Our stories are identical without even having to think. They may have won that round, but the pressure is now on them to convince the court that they were honest. There's no way I can lose the next round. Doesn't matter how good someone is at lying you can't beat someone that's telling the truth.

There will always be a mistake or a visible doubt in the testimony.

Committing perjury in court can have severe consequences. Misleading the court with false accusations and testimony is a criminal offence. It's more severe within criminal law than family law, but judges don't take kindly to being manipulated. Judge Mitchel had decided to suspend contact based on a false accusation. I don't think he will be too happy to find out that Jessie had to suffer needlessly.

Shelly had been kind enough to take time away from her family commitments to accompany me to the court hearing. She has been supportive. Always available to talk on the phone, have me visit and stay, attend court and do handovers. She has been a godsend for me. On my way home, I stopped in Norfolk to take her home, then decided to stay the night to save an arduous and continuous journey. She was happy for me to stay longer, but after court, I always want to get home so I can prepare for the ensuing battle. I can't settle until I know that I am fully equipped and done everything needed.

Upon discussing the court outcome with family and friends while I was in Norfolk, they were appalled. The decision of the court made no sense to anyone that heard the story. There was a feeling of disgust from everyone of Casey's actions, her mother's involvement and the judge's decision to suspend contact. None of it was justified.

Shelly and I behaved impeccably throughout the contact with Jessie. Shelly was polite towards Casey even though it wasn't easy for her. To witness my ex-partner causing such disruption between Jessie and I wasn't easy. When Shelly was a teenager, she was the rough brute of the family. Getting into fights and even beating up boys to protect friends. She's mellowed a lot since she has become older and has a family of her own. It was good that she was able to be cordial with Casey; I didn't want any animosity between anyone. It wouldn't help. Upsetting or hurting Casey wasn't on my agenda.

Arriving home was a relief. The drive back from Norfolk allowed me to contemplate what had happened. My mind constantly in the process of calculating potential outcomes always to be a step ahead of everyone else. Almost like a robot visualising everything. By now, my mind was exhausted.

The next morning, I immediately got to work on my statement in readiness for the court hearing. I always prepare well in advance of the filing dates. It's better to write when everything remains fresh in mind. Feelings and emotions can diminish over time. It's important to explain everything to the court. My statement took longer than usual to complete as I was contending with severe depression.

It was an emotional battle getting through the time between Jessie's abduction to the point where contact commenced. A very dark period in my life. I always found the light and fought through it, but it certainly wasn't easy. Some days were brutal. I couldn't even gain the willpower to rise from the bed. Other days involved random naps even at the most inopportune times. I could be preparing statements or searching through evidence, but there was no control over the depression. My mind shut down against my will, rendering me useless and exhausted. The naps were a regular occurrence. I powered through and persevered with the statements and evidence whenever my body would allow. As time went on, I regained my strength and learnt how to overcome the dark energy and bring the positive light back into my life.

I didn't need therapy. Well, in all honesty, I think I did. Without specialist help, I guess it just took me a little longer to return to myself of old. The break in contact made me severely relapse. Visited the doctors to explain my situation. Broke down in tears telling my story. They provided medication and recommended therapy. I acknowledged a consideration to investigate the treatment but we both knew if Jessie comes home, my troubles will disappear. I'm a fighter, though. I won't give up, no matter how hard it gets. Therapy can wait for now. I don't want it. I want Jessie back.

Medication worried me. I had witnessed Casey rely on pills during our relationship. She often missed doses for an excessive amount of time. Her mood would fluctuate to the point of dangerous for her safety. I didn't want that happening to me. In my mind, this is just temporary. What's the point of taking medication when I don't need it for long? It may or may not have helped. Either way, I just refused to submit myself to it. I endured the suffering and overcame it with an eagerness to be at my best for Jessie. I'm no use to her feeling down or sorry for myself. It won't help get her home. The only way to stand a chance is to be at my very best and show everyone how great I am as her father. I had to be the best me ever.

My parents wanted an update on everything that had happened. They were shocked that contact has stopped. Like me, they had hoped that Jessie would come home to visit soon. That dream couldn't be further away — a stark contrast to the court hearing just a couple of weeks ago where she almost came home.

They could see the torment on my face: the exhaustion and mental anguish I had to endure. I was stressed with an uncertain future. Jessie stuck in the middle of a never-ending conflict between her parents. My stepdad had previously defended Casey's parents whenever I would speak negatively about them — explaining that what would I expect them to do. Of course, they will support Casey and do everything they have to do for her. He missed the point I was trying to make. It's my opinion that Carly instigated Casey's decision to abduct Jessie. I understand a parent being protective, etc. It wasn't protecting just purely selfish without any compassion or care for the welfare or emotions of the children.

Something finally snapped inside of him. Hearing everything and witnessing what has happened, Casey's parent's attendance at court, and contact stopping so soon after it had commenced. A wave of anger had built inside. He was fuming, absolutely disgusted with Casey's mother. Not one to usually use profanity he let out the frustration, not holding back.

"Don't ever let that bitch near her again." He said in disgust.

"I can't keep her from Casey."

"Not her. The mother."

"I can't stop Casey from doing that, but I won't ever place her near her myself.", I promised.

If he could see everything that is happening and finally realise how involved Carly is in this mess, then hopefully other people will see it for themselves too. It's been so difficult to agree on anything with Casey because she has a narcissistic voice in her head — her mother.

21

FIFTH COURT HEARING

My stepdad's health had been deteriorating rapidly since contact between Jessie and me had stopped. I think the stress of the situation seriously affected his health. The medication was withdrawn in August, so his decline was inevitable anyway. The sadness for us was that clearly, time was running out to get Jessie home to see him before it's too late. The odds weren't in our favour. To date, we've only spent time together twice. Both occasions were with limited time and restricted to remain in the city she currently resides.

I arrived at court with Shelly, intrigued as to whether Casey's mum will be in attendance. I know she intended to obstruct my contact with Jessie and then return home having achieved her mission. The contested hearing on my behalf wasn't something she would've anticipated. Now she's expected to be in court with the rest of us. My sister regularly accompanies me, so her summons isn't an inconvenience for us. We're ready to provide oral testimony to the judge and face cross-examination. It is a real court hearing where we will all be under pressure to expose any weaknesses in our version of events.

After a long time of waiting, the reality was predictable. Casey's mum isn't coming to court. There was a ridiculous excuse that she isn't well. It didn't come as a shock. I would've been more surprised if she had attended.

I often try to put myself in the position of others to better understand the bigger picture. If someone is hell-bent on being disruptive and their agenda is to obstruct contact between a father and daughter, then she did well at the previous hearing. The accusations in that regard were a success. Flip it on the other side though she wouldn't fancy sitting in front of a judge. In a court of law and be subjected to a barrage of questions about her dishonesty. Her story was constantly changing. She wouldn't hold up well at all.

At the previous court hearing, Casey's mother hadst stated that she was present during the return handover after the second contact session. Shelly's witness statement since then has contradicted her version of events. Only herself, Casey and the children were present. Carly's witness statement had changed the story. Now she witnessed the events at her hotel after the contact had concluded.

It's my view that as soon as a story changes once, it can't be trusted. It was pathetic, but Casey's mother didn't expect to be questioned when the comments were made. I was here to win. It's OK to lose some court hearings. Difficult to win them all. The most import one is the final hearing. Until then, I have to do my best to keep the contact consistent and generous. It's crucial that Jessie and I can have a real relationship. Not limited and un-natural.

The appointed CAFCASS officer Margaret spoke to Casey and me separately. During my meeting with her, I explained the circumstances and the importance of Jessie's education.

I came to tears upon speaking about Casey and explaining the problems she contended with when we lived together. I often struggled to compose myself when I remembered her vulnerability. Regardless of whether she now hates me, I still had a deep love for her. I just wanted her to be safe and look after herself. Margaret explained her views and that she was in favour of Jessie and me having a generous amount of contact together. It was her opinion that the more contact, the better.

Without her mother here for support or more pertinently interference; Casey changed her stance. Now she was allowing unsupervised contact to recommence. I wasn't impressed. If she was honourable, we could have avoided this court hearing, which would've saved my legal fees and all the disruption. It was blatantly apparent that she was protecting herself from suffering the ordeal of being cross-examined in court. Now she can appear to be positive and working to resolve ongoing issues which looks favourable to a judge. It's all a facade to resemble the great mother she wishes to portray. The reality is much darker and sinister. I had to contend with a malevolent evil. The devil incarnate, hell-bent on being disruptive and detrimental while appearing to be perfect on the outside. I had been ready for my turn in court, but how can I justify not accepting contact? There was little choice but to proceed with the new arrangements.

One would think that being on the back foot and fortunately avoiding an embarrassing cross-examination that Casey would be grateful for the opportunity to move on positively. Nope. Not Casey. I don't think she fully grasps the situations in court. Her proposals again are concise contact sessions. How on earth is that a progression from what I had previously?

I wonder what it must be like for her legal representatives having to explain everything and try and reason with her. It must be an absolute nightmare. I can picture her simply saying no contact — no way, not a full day. I bet the three-hour suggestions to them are a miracle. Then it gets presented to me, and I am absolute in my refusal to accept anything that isn't in Jessie's best interests.

My only thought is Jessie, and whether she would be happy with that? If the answer is no, then I refuse. It's rather simple. That is how I know that Casey decides everything with only her best interests in mind. If she were thinking of Jessie, we would have no problems agreeing. Instead, we are opposites. May as well be on the other side of the planet. We can't agree on anything.

During negotiations, it became evident to me that Casey is going to be obstructive at every opportunity. The video recordings she captured of Jessie upset were inappropriate. Watching the recordings was difficult to endure. Casey was interrogating Jessie for information and had no interest in comforting with a cuddle. She was leading answers herself and getting Jessie to agree with what she's saying. Casey's behaviour wasn't sincere, promising not to tell anyone what Jessie says and providing guarantees of regular contact. Casey can't be trusted as she did tell everyone by using the videos against me, which negatively affected Jessie. The entire situation is ridiculous.

While talking to my Miss Choi, I asked, "Can we put a stop to further video recordings in future. It shouldn't be happening. It's just disruptive."

"That's a good point. I'll raise it in the hearing."

Lucky that it came to mind; otherwise, situations like this will likely occur regularly. Everything was agreed between Casey and I finally although we still conflicted over the end time of contact. I wanted an extra hour. Casey refused. Miss Choi suggested that I accept her proposals. She made the point that she knows the judge.

"He won't give you the hour at best he'll split it down the middle."

"That's still an extra 30 minutes. Might not mean anything to Casey but every minute matters to Jessie and me."

"OK, we'll leave it to the judge."

Low and behold, the judge did as expected, provided the extra thirty minutes. Victory. That was worth the effort. I must fight for every inch. The order was made that there be no further video recordings by either party. Judge Mitchel made a valid point

"There's no benefit to the proceedings in capturing video. The child may have been provoked before the start of the recording."

It was a result for me and a good day. I had hoped for weekend contact, but I have already learnt that I need to take the court proceedings slowly. Need to walk before I run. Just follow the procedure, and I'll get there eventually.

CAFCASS were provided with an extension to file the S7 report by the 20th November 2017. Casey and I are required to register position statements in response to the S7 report by the 2nd December 2017. Whichever parent the report favours will have a significant bearing on where Jessie will permanently reside when court proceedings conclude.

For now, the situation is weekly phone calls at 6 pm and fortnightly contact in Liverpool. The first session 11 am to 4 pm and then the following two contacts are to be from 11 am to 6.30pm. A bonus is that Casey is bringing her eldest daughter Emma to Chelmsford to visit family for the half-term holidays. As Jessie will be accompanying them on the journey, I made the point in court that it would benefit her to spend some time with my family and me. To my surprise, it was accepted. Casey wanted just an hour. I received three hours. Not amazing, considering we still need to drive back and forth from the train station. So really, it's only two hours. Handover in Chelmsford is to be done by Casey's friend Sarah. Shelly doesn't reside near me, and it's my hometown, so it's for Casey to avoid me rather than have me stay clear.

For the avoidance of doubt, it was explained, I am still bound by the previously signed declaration to return Jessie at the end of each contact. Both parents are to refrain from speaking negatively of the other in Jessie's presence. That's sensible and fair though Casey isn't used to following rules, so I didn't hold out much hope of her behaving.

I'm not permitted to ask Jessie about which school she attends or her residence. The rules I had to abide by were getting pathetic. It baffled me. Safeguarding reports came back clear, yet I'm still treated as a potential abuser as the situation hasn't been fully explored in court. There were contradictions. I can't know the name of the school, but I can talk about her school progress. Absolute madness. It's like a minefield of conversation to explore while also being careful not to reveal sensitive information, how this is in Jessie's best interests' beggar's belief. The only person that gains anything is Casey, and even then, I'm not sure what. She lives miles away. The other end of the country. It's hardly a risk that I could find myself within the vicinity of her home or school on non-contact days. All I can do is focus on Jessie and leave Casey to play games. Hopefully, she will trip herself up, and everyone will eventually see for themselves the madness I've had to endure.

22

RETURNING HOME

My little girl was coming home for the first time since all of this happened. She had been away for far too long. Casey had concocted a story of me smashing up our home to Jessie. I can show her the flat, and she can see for herself that it's how she left it. I had made some minor changes during all this upheaval. Emma's bed dismantled and passed onto Shelly for her son. It was a lovely white cabin bed with pull out desk which he would enjoy. It's identical to Jessie's. My mum had purchased the beds for the kids, so it was my choice what to do with them. Emma won't be returning, so there was no need for two beds to remain in a modestly sized bedroom. Removing it provides Jessie with plenty of extra room for her to play. The bonus is that she won't be burdened by memories of us all living together when she returns. It's a chance for a fresh start, just the two of us.

Oddly before everyone had left, Casey and I never got around to placing photos on the walls. It was as though we had just regarded the flat as a temporary dwelling. Living on my own, I wanted Jessie to be near me, so I purchased fancy photo frames that allow multiple photo combinations. The living room was now a family room with recent memories of Jessie and I. Emma is included in a couple of the photos though I didn't include any of Casey. It wasn't to block her from Jessie's life when she is with me; it is to prevent her from mine when she isn't. Casey is the past which I want to forget.

Arriving at the train station to collect Jessie was confusing. It was the first time we were to handover here. It was difficult to know where they will be waiting. The only information provided was Chelmsford train station. That seemed simple enough before I arrived. Now that I am here, there's no knowing where to wait — arriving early just complicated things further. I was always walking back and forth from one side to the other desperate not to miss them or cause any delays. Having Jessie home was too precious. We need all the time together we can have. The family are waiting at my parents' house to see her. Before then I need to whisk Jessie off home so she can be back for the first time and open the birthday presents I had been waiting for months to provide.

I was waiting for Casey's friend Sarah. She drives a white van, so I kept a lookout everywhere. My phone rang unexpectedly. I didn't recognise the phone number and always ignored unsolicited calls. It was almost certain to be regarding this handover, so I accepted the call. To my surprise, it was Casey calling.

"Hi Steve, it's Casey, can we meet to talk?"

"Yeah, that's fine."

"Do you want me to come to you or you come to me?"

"I can walk to you; it's no problem."

"I'm at the car park by Sarah's van."

"I see it. I'll see you in a minute."

The call ended. I wasn't expecting this. She had made me out to be a lunatic for months. Even now, I don't know if she genuinely believes what she says or whether she knows it's nonsense. If she was fearful of me, then I am surprised that she wants to speak in person. I can't even be near her in Liverpool to collect Jessie. Even today, it was her friend scheduled to take care of the handover in her absence.

Upon catching sight of Casey for the first time in public since this all started, I provided a welcoming smile. I wanted her to be at ease and not feel any discomfort. Her actions have hurt me profoundly but beating that to death won't help anyone.

"Hi, I want you to know that I'm fine. There's no animosity from me." I explained

"Can we sort this out between us?"

I noticed that Jessie was too close in proximity to Casey and able to listen to the conversation.

"Jessie can hear us. Could you move her back or let her wait with Sarah while we talk?"

"Go there for a minute." Casey motioned for Jessie to step back.

"What do you have in mind?" I asked.

"Can we sort it all out without legal teams?"

"I don't see why not. If you come back to Chelmsford, then I would agree to 50/50 custody."

"I'm staying in Liverpool."

"What do you propose then?"

"Jessie lives with me, and you can have half of the holidays."

"I can't do that. Jessie needs to come home to me. You can have all the holidays."

It was apparent we weren't going to be able to agree. The positive at least is that we have been able to engage in dialogue with one another. We both understand each other's demands, and at this moment in time, neither party is prepared to lower their requirements for custody. The hurtful thing for Jessie and I is that Casey's body language and tone indicated that had I agreed to holidays then she would've allowed Jessie to remain with me for the half-term holiday. Emma is staying nearby in the holidays with her father. As we hadn't agreed, we remain restricted by a three-hour limited contact arrangement. Jessie is to then return with Casey to Liverpool after. It wasn't fair on her at all — no consideration of Jessie's feelings or desires. A mother was playing games to get what she wants. It hurts me, but I need to remain composed and focus on the long-term. In the grand scheme of things, this setback will be worth it. I hope.

I hugged Jessie and walked with her to my car. She was excited to be coming back home. The smile was glued to her face. Nothing would ruin this moment for her. The car journey was fun and silly. We hadn't been in a car together for so long. We laughed a lot and had so much fun. It's as though we had never been away from each other — an instant connection and totally in sync.

When we got home, I hadn't anticipated Jessie being like a kid in a sweet shop. I had a schedule all planned out. She is to open presents and then we need to get to my parents' home to see the family. Especially her granddad as he is ill, and it means so much to him to see her again. He may never get another opportunity. Jessie was opening presents but then walking around in-between rooms after each gift opened. Her mind wouldn't concentrate on anything. She was eager to view every part of our home and see everything that she had to leave behind.

It was a very emotional moment for her. She gave me regular cuddles and affection. We knew we both loved each other immensely. We didn't need to show it, but we did it anyway. She is the epicentre of my world. Her happiness is my everything. It was great to witness her smiling, but then it would soon disappear and come back. She was conflicted. Happy to be home but sad that it's only for a short while.

I had to focus Jessie on the task at hand. Reaffirmed that we need to get to nannies after as everyone's waiting to see her. She loved them all but didn't want to leave our home. She cherished the moment and the life we have together. I assured her we would be back soon enough. We won't always be in Liverpool.

We arrived at my parents' home after a short drive just a couple of miles away. Their home was a big part of Jessie's life. Most of her childhood had been spent visiting weekends, after school and holidays. As mentioned previously, we had also resided at their home for nine months. It's like a home from home.

Walking through the front door was reminiscent of a birthday party. Jessie greeted by so many familiar faces welcoming her home. Mum, Oakley, Lee, Kerrie, David and Rustler the dog which Casey and I had rescued and re-homed with my parents. Jessie loves my parents, but there's one person that gets her excited. My nephew and Jessie's cousin Oakley. He adores Jessie, and she glows when he is around. They are best friends, and it's been hard on them both to be separated. The courts don't consider the other family members, aside from siblings. Jessie is closer to Oakley than her sister. They are the same age; well, Jessie is eight months older and different years of school. Witnessing them playing together is brilliant. They're both usually eager to include me within their antics.

My stepdad had deteriorated significantly. The decision was made a few weeks ago that children in the family will be kept away as it's not appropriate for them to witness him so poorly. It will affect them too much. I was conflicted with Jessie. Even the day before her arrival, I told my mum that I think I'll keep her away. Whose best interests do I serve? I can't do the right thing for everyone. Jessie always comes first in my life, but I was at crossroads. She is a strong and brave girl. More mature than her age suggests. I had to weigh up whether she would be able to cope with witnessing him so fragile and poorly. A man that has always been the strong pillar of the family. Now he is a shell of the man he once was. It could be traumatising for Jessie to witness such a drastic change.

I couldn't pass up the chance to make my stepdad happy. It meant the world to him to see her again as it is for him with all the children in our family. He hadn't seen her in a long time considering she regularly visited before her abduction. While his health declined over recent months; he was very involved within my legal battle providing his opinions and thoughts. He was devoted as always to maintain our family. Sadly, he won't be here for a conclusion as court proceedings are slow and unnecessarily drawn out. His time on this earth was quickly diminishing.

I called out to Jessie to temporarily stop her playing with Oakley. My stepdad often gets exhausted and tired. He was currently alert enough to greet Jessie. I walked her into my parents' bedroom. He already had family surrounding him as we all popped in on him regularly to make sure he's comfortable. I asked Jessie if she would like to hug him. She reacted with a comforting cuddle.

"Hello, darling." He said softly.

"Hi, granddad. I love you."

"Love you too."

It was a brief encounter. Jessie's northern accent had everyone intrigued, and it amused my stepdad. He felt that she sounded adorable. I could sense discomfort in Jessie from witnessing her granddad so frail, so I excused her from the room. She told him that she loves him. He was thrilled to have seen her again. He liked the kids to play and be able to hear them. Never one to usually have a fuss for himself, so he was okay with their meeting being brief. It was difficult to see him look so different. Jessie maintained a positive composure and remained polite. She behaved impeccably. I was incredibly proud of her. She wasn't aware of how poorly he was or the severity. All she knew was that he is ill. I never indicated to her at any point that he's near death. She didn't need to know that. If she had known, I'm sure that she would've hugged him much longer, but she would've been traumatised. There was no benefit in her knowing. He knows she loves him.

Jessie and Oakley went outside to play in the garden. They enjoy playing hide-and-seek, although the places to hide are somewhat limited. They find each too quickly so harassed me to join them. Both were wanting to be out of sight and for me to look for them. I agreed, much to their delight. The funny thing about playing with them is that they tend to either hide in locations which fail to conceal them or Oakley giggles. Jessie will laugh sometimes, but Oakley often struggles to maintain his composure. He gets so excited.

I make a lot of noise, pretending not to know where they are. Struggling to locate them and go to places I know they aren't to prolong the game. There's no fun in finding someone immediately. Even when I got close to them, I still act as though I can't see them and walk away a failure. They both giggle. They often hide next to each other, which means that one always struggles to remain hidden. When I finally find them, they are both amazed and amused that it took me so long. They must think I'm stupid. Both end up with smiles on their faces having enjoyed themselves.

I looked at the time on my phone concerned that I will arrive late at the train station for Jessie's return. I told her that we need to go in a minute so she needs to say her goodbyes as we can't be late. It was abrupt, and she was distraught. She was finally home with the family she adored. My family had been more prominent and consistent throughout her life than Casey's. Even Casey had spent more time with my family than hers. It's hardly a surprise that she would miss everyone, and now that they are back in her life it's taken away again. I'm bound by the court to return her promptly. I couldn't afford to violate the order. Oakley was distressed along with Jessie. He couldn't understand why she must leave. None of the situation made sense to him. I had to be firm though. I keep fighting to get her home, but I need to be perfect throughout. No mistakes.

While waiting at the traffic lights just down the road from my parents' home, I asked my brother what the time is. In my eagerness to be punctual I think I got the time wrong.

"4"

"She isn't due back until 5.30! We're going back to mums."

Jessie was crying and laughing at the same time. It was emotional and confusing for her. She was behaving like Harley Quinn from the Batman series. She was relieved not to be going back just yet.

Everyone was surprised to see us all returning. Oakley was thrilled. He gave Jessie a big hug and smiled with joy. I explained that I got the time wrong. Lee offered to go and get the kids McDonald's so that I don't have to be separated from her and Jessie can stay and play with Oakley. I thanked him for the gesture.

When the living room was empty, I picked Jessie up and gave her a big hug. She cuddled me and came close to tears. It had been an emotional day for her. It was clear that she missed the life she adored. It wasn't her decision to move up north away from everyone she knew. Her entire life changed in an instant. It must be hard for her to endure. Powerless to alter her own life and be happy.

She knows that I'm fighting for her and that I've made some progress as she's here now. Mum walked into the room but could see that we were having an emotional moment together so walked back out without Jessie knowing. It was a heartbreaking moment. I was bound by rules to follow, which we shouldn't have to adhere. Nothing was just or fair. I put her back down and gave her a tap on the shoulder and said, "I love you". She composed herself and went to play with Oakley. It was nice that they get an extra hour together. For them, it was a bonus — a moment to savour.

Jessie spent some time trying on clothes that mum had bought. She regularly gets the kids new clothes from Next on her store card. During the time that Jessie had been away, there was a bag filled with new clothes collected and ready for her to wear. Jessie was now the human doll constantly changing clothes to see if everything fits and to her liking. A white outfit had her smitten, so she left it on. A pink cardigan provided a beautiful contrast to the clothes set. As she isn't home with me yet consistently, I'm allowing the clothes to return with her to Liverpool. She's growing so fast. They won't fit for very long, so it's better that she be able to enjoy wearing them as much as possible.

Lee arrived with the McDonalds later than expected. It wasn't for lack of effort. The drive-thru queue was longer than anticipated. After the earlier episode of me demanding haste, Jessie was trying to rush eating her food. I calmed her down and encouraged her to relax and enjoy it. If need be, we can take it with us for her to eat in the car. For now, we have time remaining as we don't have to leave for a few minutes yet. Secretly I was hoping that Casey would message me to allow Jessie to stay for the holidays. It was becoming clear that that's not going to happen.

I drove Jessie back to the train station. The mood wasn't as fun on the return. There was a feeling of farewell as opposed to joy. We both knew that our time together was coming to an end. Despair and dread were setting in. Upon arriving at the train station, Jessie was visibly anxious. Her sister Emma wasn't present as she was remaining in Chelmsford. Only her mother was there to greet her. Jessie and I said our goodbyes with a kiss and a cuddle then they walked off together into the train station with Jessie in floods of tears. She was inconsolable.

For the first time, Jessie and I will be having weekly phone calls. It is to be a permanent part of our relationship between the fortnightly contact sessions. The first call took place during the Autumn half-term holidays. Emma was away staying with family.

To my surprise, the call was clearly on the loudspeaker. There's a noticeable difference in sound quality and volume. I deplore conference calls. There's no freedom to communicate directly or be sure who's listening in to the conversation.

I remained polite about the situation and didn't raise any concerns at the time. Casey was present throughout the call. Jessie had something on her mind, which she wanted to discuss with me.

"Daddy, can I get my ears pierced?" Jessie asked.

"Yeah, that's fine if mummy agrees."

"She said I could."

"Then you can, can't you," I replied

"Who's taking her?" Casey interrupted.

"It's up to you; I don't mind," I said in response.

"Jessie can choose who she wants to take her," Casey suggested.

"I want daddy," Jessie said with confidence.

"That's fine then. I'll take her, though I don't know where to go to have them done."

"You can get them done at Clair's. They do piercings." Casey explained.

"Oh OK. Thanks for letting me know. We'll go there then."

The topic soon changed to the new clothes Jessie had bought back with her upon returning to Liverpool.

"The clothes Jessie bought back are really nice. Are any of them Emma's?"

"Yeah. She looks beautiful in them. We were going to get Emma clothes but didn't know the situation."

"It's up to you. I just wondered if any of the clothes Jessie bought back were for Emma."

"Ok. We'll then if it's fine I'll make sure to get her some clothes too."

Jessie went on to explain that she has a corpse bride costume for Halloween. She was excited and enjoyed dressing up. It's one of her favourite holiday periods. Casey does well with face painting the kids. I'm always impressed with her efforts. The character the kids are portraying comes to life.

The conversation was cordial between Casey and me. It was disrespectful though to force the call to be a conference. Jessie and I shouldn't have restrictions on our telephone call. There was no such instruction within the court order. Casey was controlling and intrusive.

I sent an update of the phone call to my solicitors immediately after the call had ended. I was irritated by the loudspeaker. It shouldn't be happening and needs to stop before next week's call. I didn't want animosity between Casey and me, but she needs to follow the same rules that I have to abide. If she wished for restrictions, then she should have made those requests in court. There's no way a judge would approve of such measures. It forces an un-natural conversation as there's an inability to speak freely and in confidence.

23

R.I.P.

Within ten days of Jessie's visit, my stepdad passed away. I was at home after shopping in my local B&Q store to purchase a new light bulb for the bathroom. After leaving the store, I was at odds whether to visit my parents or go home. I had been attending daily, so I felt a day to myself would be best on this occasion. I received a phone call within an hour of being home and fitting the new light bulb. My stepdad had passed away.

There had been plenty of family members around him before his passing. He had suffered enough. Battling and contending with progressive cancer for much longer than doctors and nurses expected. Over a month longer than anticipated. He is a fighter and a true family man. It's believed that he had wanted to see everyone and most importantly, to know that my mum will be fine without him. He had been waiting to hear from her that she will be OK. After receiving that reassurance, he waited for everyone to leave the bedroom to have their dinner. When they left, he took his leave from this world.

I had made the wrong decision returning home when I should have gone to visit. There's nothing I could've done, and we had a good heart to heart recently. I told him how much I love him, and he told me too. Beyond my daughter,

I'm not an affectionate person. With her, it comes naturally. I didn't realise that he had wanted a hug from me. Mum had to tell me so of course I was happy to do it and that's when we had our private conversation.

At the beginning of October, all my family came together to be there for my stepdad. Brothers flew in from abroad. Some of us remain local while a couple of them made new lives for themselves in exotic locations. It was great to have everyone coming together. My sister Kerrie and I had been at war for a long time. A few years more than we really should. I was protective of Casey and always favoured her in an argument. There had been an issue between us in this regard, which neither would forgive the other. It had been my stepdad's dying wish for everyone to get along and forgive. As with all families, there are issues to resolve. It wasn't easy for us to move on. We tried our best but often failed with regular remarks towards each other. In the end, we both saw sense and moved forward in peace. We should never have been at war in the first place.

There were a few niggling issues between my stepbrothers and mum, along with a few other people. I was always the peacemaker. The one caught in the middle between both sides. I didn't like any preferential treatment and understood the issues everyone had with the other. After some time, peace restored, and everyone was able to be together. It's a relatively small accommodation for so many adults to be in at a given moment. I enjoyed having everyone together and would've loved for it to be like this all the time.

Our family is huge with seven siblings, all with their partners and children. It's impossible to get everyone together regularly. Especially those that reside abroad in Spain and America. Family members that can afford the travel visit for holidays. Those that live close by keep in regular contact and spend time together when we can. We're a close family that has been raised well to always be there for one another.

My brothers are physically stronger than I. I'm the tech geek of the family though I'm no pushover and will stand up for myself. My stepbrother Cody suggested feeding Casey to crocodiles in Florida.

"She'll never be found."

"That sounds lovely, but I wouldn't want to hurt her. I just want Jessie home."

"Solves the problem."

"Doesn't really though does it. Jessie wouldn't have her mother."

I want to think he was joking, but I think he was serious. Slightly worrying but I never wish Casey to be hurt. Not only is she the mother of my child, which I hold dear regardless of her behaviour. Deep down, I will always love her. I spent our entire relationship, protecting her and even fighting my own family in her honour. She was my world. Just because she chooses to hurt me now and our daughter too, I wouldn't take any joy from her suffering.

I rushed around to mums home immediately after receiving the phone call. Everyone was in tears, struggling to come to terms with the finality of what has happened. He won't be here anymore. All we have now are memories. I don't tend to process things like everyone else. My sister Kerrie is very emotional, so she expresses herself immediately. My mum was inconsolable as were others present. My stepbrother Ryan arrived shortly after me. He was distraught. It affected him more than anyone. He had issues with my mum since childhood. They always seemed to be at odds with each other. His dad was his world. I process everything when I'm in private at home. For now, I'm comforting others helping them deal with the loss.

I had the opportunity to go into the bedroom to see my stepdad for one last time before the coroner arrives. I declined. I had the memories I wanted to keep. Seeing him still and breathless wasn't an image I wanted to stuck into my mind, preferring to remember him healthy and more significantly, alive.

His loss affected me a lot more than I had expected. My family have lost many members throughout the years from aunts and grandparents. Losing a parent, though, isn't something to be expected. He was still relatively young in his mid-60's. Never afforded the time to retire. He was working up until his body wouldn't allow anymore. Cancer took him away from work, not his age. He never got to enjoy the rest and rewards of his labour.

He wasn't someone that passed on compliments. More pearls of wisdom and encourage improvement. Things to do better etc. After his passing my mum told me that he had told her to say to me "Never give up getting Jessie home.

Do everything you have to." That was never in doubt. I will never give up on my daughter.

People told me after that he had referred to me as a great father. It made me incredibly proud. To know that he thought that of me was inspiring. I try my best and always put Jessie first in everything I do.

24

MENTAL HEALTH

This is the hardest moment for me to write. Sharing someone else's torment isn't without compassion. I realise that by with-holding facts, the reasons for my fear of Jessie's welfare are unclear. At the same time, I must consider other peoples privacy. It's a delicate balance, but in the end, I have decided to disclose certain information to validate those fears and rationale.

Casey has had a tormented life. Her childhood filled with a desire to gain her parent's attention. All of this was in vain as she isn't the most patient and often feels neglected and unwanted. She jumped from one relationship to another to fill the void. I can't say with any certainty whether her family were supportive when she was a child or not. All I know is what she told me. Though judging by the past few years and lies of abuse, it should be taken with some scepticism.

When we first met, Casey was rather shy and vulnerable. She lacked confidence. Her boyfriend, considerably older and future father of Emma, had been cheating on her. Well, at least that's what she told me. They often went out weekends though not together, which I found rather strange. However, it's not for me to pass judgement. If true, then her lack of confidence would make sense added to the lack of attention she received from her family as a child.

A few months after I left the job, we shared she sent me a text message explaining that she is worried she's pregnant. Casey had no ambition to be a mother. It worried her immensely. She was confiding in me as I was a friendly voice that doesn't judge. I reassured her that it would be OK. I encouraged her to be more careful in future after she got the all clear that it was a false alarm. A month or so later, she would go on to be pregnant. She was now carrying her baby Emma. Our lives naturally drifted apart.

2009 was the year we would re-connect. I had hoped to find her again one day. She had been on my mind a lot for the past few years although our contact information had changed with no way to get in touch. Eventually, I found her on Facebook after searching through a mutual friend's, friend list. I sent her a message, and we re-engaged with one another. Eventually meeting up and having a great time. It was apparent that her life was in disarray. She told me how she had left Emma with her parents for three months as she couldn't cope. Her father struggled to deal with the trauma and had a heart attack. He recovered. Casey stayed with her cousin in Kent while she tried to figure out what to do with her life. She was now contemplating leaving again as failed relationships haunted her.

When our relationship commenced, I was sure that it would last the test of time. I adored her, and I know Casey loved me too. Emma was already three years old. Having a child of my own meant the world to me. It was everything.

I didn't want to have a child that has such a vast difference in age to Emma. It was vital that they be able to have a close relationship. Casey didn't want more children. She barely coped with the one she already had. It's important not to confuse this with not wanting Emma as she loves her immensely. That much is certain. Love isn't the issue; it's the demons in her mind of which she must contend. She struggled to cope with Emma's desire to be with the father. She was confiding in me that she can't do it anymore. She intends just to let her live with him. I explained that she would live to regret that decision. She took my advice and didn't impulsively abandon Emma. It's natural for a child to miss the other parent when they see very little of them and only in short bursts. It's essential not to take it personally.

Emma and I got on wonderfully. I played with her regularly and helped nurture and teach. She was often rude to me upon returning from her father but would soon get back into the usual routine. She was a demanding child and didn't like to share. Before Jessie's arrival, there weren't other children in her life to share and play. She had everyone to herself whenever she wanted. I never gave up on her, always supporting her achievements.

In the same way, I am with Jessie I encourage their best efforts, manners and not to take life too seriously. Jessie is very carefree, strong-willed, friendly and polite. Emma is less likely to share, bossy and neurotic. It's not to say she doesn't have fun and be silly though it just doesn't come naturally. She is very similar to Casey. Casey's family often refer to her as a mini-Casey.

Casey became pregnant in August 2009. She was tormented. Uncertain whether to proceed with the pregnancy or terminate. I tried to be supportive. After all, it's her body. She's the one that must endure the physical demands and exhaustion. We did have arguments with differing points of view. I was conflicted for sure. Made it clear that if she does abort then our relationship is over. Not out of spite or anything petty. Simply if my child were terminated then I wouldn't be able to look at her anymore physically. If it's her wish, then I felt obliged to support her. She would hold this moment against me for the entirety of our relationship. Regularly saying to me "You only stayed for Jessie. You don't love me." It affected her more than it should. I'd explained my reason countless times. I loved her immensely. She was the one I'm meant to be with, though taking my child, is more than I could bear. Of course, she would go onto take her away from me anyway years later though the circumstances are different.

I drove Casey to a clinic in north London. The car journey was tense. She only changed her mind at the very last moment outside the clinic after talking to her mother on the phone. I have no idea what she said. Casey made it clear to me that she is having this child for me and that it'll be up to me to do everything as she doesn't want to go through it all again. I agreed to take on all responsibility. This meant the world to me.

The pregnancy was difficult with Casey regularly collapsing for no apparent reason. I always supported her and made sure she's comfortable and rested. I've heard a lot of women have uncomplicated pregnancies. I can confirm that for Casey, it was brutal. Her body and mind were drained and exhausted. She had always relied on drinking alcohol and smoking to help her relax. I did my best to stop that until Jessie is born to provide her with the best chance of development. It's only years later when I realised that there was a correlation between the withdrawal of these habits about the decline in her mental health.

When Jessie was born, I was proud of both Casey and her. This beautiful baby is part of us both. Casey had been exhausted. Giving birth laying down with gas wasn't working. Her hair was dripping with sweat. I was worried about her health. Eventually, she was moved from the bed into a sitting position to encourage the baby to be delivered. Casey held onto my hands and squeezed with an incredible force which hurt immensely. I'm sure the pain I felt was hardly anything in comparison to what she had endured. I was scared for Casey so much so that I refused to hold Jessie until I knew she was okay. I spoke to her mum on the phone explaining the situation. She was confident that Casey would be OK. Upon holding Jessie for the first time, my life changed in an instant. This tiny person was now my biggest priority in life.

Fast forward a few years and the excitement and euphoria of our new relationship was waning. Life had slowed and settled into a monotonous and somewhat scripted domestic lifestyle. I was happy with the life we had. Of course, raising children is challenging and often exhausting. I wouldn't change it for the world. Casey pined for the freedom and carefree life she had before kids. She enjoyed drinking with no responsibilities. I never restricted or prevented her from weekends out with friends. She was free to do as she wants. The conflict for her was that she missed that lifestyle but was at crossroads in her life where she no longer found it enjoyable. There was a desire to have her youth back and almost go back in time.

Before our relationship, I had been able to do as and what I wanted when I wanted as I wasn't tied down by bonds or children. I did, however, bear the responsibility of my young nephew as my brother was lethargic without any interest in being a role model. I took him to the park and on bike-rides through nearby woods and days out at the zoo. Nurturing children has always been a big part of my character. I have many nieces and nephews, and they often regard me as their favourite uncle.

Casey was thrust into something she had no desire to do or be. Being a parent wasn't on her list of life goals. Her frustrations are understandable, but there must come the point where she must accept the hand that has been dealt. Children grow up, and then there's all the time in the world to do all the things missed out. Well, that's how I see it at least. It's hard to get someone that often feels sorry for themselves to see anything other than the drama they envisage.

We had a difficult struggle to remain in our private rented home due to the landlord wishing to sell the property. I did all I could to prolong the inevitable. With nowhere else to go, I had little choice but to fight through the court. Casey found it exhausting and gave up fighting. I had to finish the battle for us. In some ways, it was a success as it did take a couple of years to move us on finally.

When the time came to pack our belongings and put furniture into storage, Casey had a breakdown. Refusing to help and gave up. She couldn't handle the stress of life. Ready to walk out and leave it all behind. I had to encourage her to see sense and help get everything packed so I can take it to storage. It was impossible to get it all done in time on my own.

Thankfully sense was knocked into her, and she gained an enthusiasm to get everything packed. During our time living at my parents' home, I started having to take Casey to the doctors for help with her mental health issues. At our bungalow, over the years she has suffered from depression and anxiety, which I always did my best to help though never truly understood what bought it on or how to manage best. Now she was getting worse and much more frequent.

The doctors are eager to assist but seem unable to know what to do. The look of despair on their faces showed all too well that it's beyond the expertise of a GP. Help only started when Casey had a severe relapse beginning to have suicidal intentions. She knew she needed help, so asked me to take her to the hospital. We arrived with the children though I kept them shielded from what's happening — speaking softly to the receptionist of the situation. When the doctors were seeing Casey, I waited with the kids on a bench outside amongst some trees. All they knew was that mummy is seeing the doctor.

A referral from the emergency doctor started the process of professional help. It was a godsend in a moment of despair. Witnessing someone, I adored and loved so low and anguished was genuinely heartbreaking. I had done everything I could to encourage a positive outlook, but even my attempts just weren't enough. There was something much bigger traumatising her I couldn't work it out myself.

At home, Casey was beginning to behave strange and impulsive, pinching herself to test her pain threshold and tying her clothing tightly around her wrists. I was scared for her. It is not her normal behaviour. Something was seriously wrong and only seeming to get worse. The long and short of it is that Casey was voluntarily sectioned at a secure mental health ward of a hospital. I had found her in the garage hiding a dog lead behind her back. I instinctively knew to look for her. Upon seeing her distressed with the lead I knew that that was the moment she could've taken her life. Something inside urged me to look for her even though I was exhausted. As a strange coincidence, the therapists who had visited Casey earlier that day phoned to check up on her. She tried to play it down as though she's okay. I asked to speak with them and told them what had happened. Casey knew she wasn't okay and needed help. What we didn't realise at the time was around this exact moment a photo of Casey flew off the wall at her parents' house. It was as though a higher purpose was looking out for her to make sure she gets the help she needs.

I visited every day and was relentless in my pursuit to get her out as per her wishes. She was desperate to come home. I was inconsolable upon arriving home after visiting Casey. My parents moved me into their bedroom to avoid the children from seeing me upset. Everyone was doing their best to shield the kids from knowing anything. It was incredibly traumatising to witness Casey on the brink. The next day while I was with Casey, her parents came to my parents' home in an attempt to take the children from their care. My mum made an excuse that the kids aren't home while they were in another room watching TV. Upon returning home, I was fuming. How dare they? What gives them the right to make such demands? I was disgusted. Rather than take the time to discuss their concerns with me, they went behind my back. All the while I am supporting their daughter through the darkest moments of her life without any support.

I proceeded to type a letter detailing everything that has happened to Casey's mother. Within the letter, I also explained how protective I am of the children, and that had she removed them, then I would've had them swiftly returned. I would go on to take Casey's mum with me to visit Casey. It was nice to see her getting the support and acceptance from her family, although it was clear that her mum didn't understand. Doctors were adamant that it's essential that the prescribed medicine must be maintained without missing doses as the side-effects are severe. It would explain the severity of her recent episodes. Doses were missed.

Casey's mother insisted to her that pills aren't the answer. She is stating that it will do her more harm than good, especially in the long term. She also researched what she needs to say to get her out of there swiftly.

- A strong support system
- Don't say I shouldn't be here as everyone says that.
- Explain that you've had time to realise what is essential and that you miss your kids.

It's this manipulation of the situation and extensive research which lead me to believe that she is heavily involved in the abduction of Jessie. She's capable of looking into everything that must be said and accused to get what they want.

It seemed to me that this was a wakeup call and now she appreciates the life she has. Casey was falling in love with me all over again, seeing for herself my commitment to her. Her mother and I had a heart to heart coming together for Casey. We were never at war with each other. I know that Casey's parents blame me for something they don't understand. Easier to have a scapegoat rather than look at the deeper issues. If they'd opened their eyes, they would see that I was continually looking out for Casey. I never tried to control her. I just wanted her to be happy. I offered Casey the opportunity to spend time with her family at the hospital, and I'll stay home, but she insisted that she only wants me.

Upon her return home, our passion for one another rekindled. We were in love again. The truth is, I've always been in love with Casey. It's her that is often conflicted and indecisive. We attended my sister Shelly's wedding a week or so after Casey's release from the hospital. Everything was going fine. She spent a night at her parents but desired to be with me even though again I insisted she does what she wants. There's no need to worry about me. She didn't want to be there. For Casey, 'home' was with me. Her mother became a negative influence confusing Casey's mind. Casey's mum insisted that she go on the housing list without me. She was trying to use abuse to justify the decision. Casey refused to declare such a notion though unsure whether to remain with me. At the time, I had no idea.

Casey had accused me of being too picky with the housing selections as the reason for our bidding suspension. I even wrote to the local MP and got him involved. The truth is that the housing department had suspended our account until Casey decided what she wants. It was very manipulative from both. I didn't know of Casey's mother's involvement or Casey's indecision until court proceedings. To think at this moment, I was trying my best to support Casey, and here I was being treated with disdain and made to believe it's my fault. It's the tip of the iceberg, and the start of the mayhem Casey's mother would begin to create.

It transpires that during our time living at my parent's home, Casey had been capturing indecent photos of herself and sending to someone. He went onto use those images to manipulate her into maintaining contact. Casey is absolute that nothing happened between them but that he began to stalk her after leaving the hospital. He is a significant bearing on why she declined so rapidly and ending up sectioned. Her mother was blaming me for the problems while Casey was hiding the truth from everyone. I only found out because this person randomly sent me a message with the photos attached — retaliation for her lack of co-operation. My reaction was to give her cuddle and let her know she's loved.

After we moved into our new flat together, things declined fast. It didn't take long for Casey's mood to drop. She was self-harming though I think for attention. Pills, knives, nooses she was a regular risk to herself. I was struggling to manage the situation. My mental wellbeing was being affected. Tired and exhausted, there's only so much someone can do. Amongst all of this, I had to keep the kids stable and unaware. I was telling them that mummies not well now, so let her rest and leave her alone for a bit. Little did they know that she was having psychotic episodes which are incredibly frightening. I wouldn't wish it on anyone. It's like something out of a horror movie.

Against my repeated requests, Casey wouldn't let me involve her family. It was more than I could handle on my own. I needed help with the situation. Casey responded that if I told any of them, then she would end it now. I had little choice but to do as she wished. Keep it to myself and do my best to support her. The frequency of these episodes was frightening. Put out one fire only to deal with it again the same day later or the next day. It was just so random with no apparent trigger. I couldn't understand how she could be so unhappy. I adored her; she had the kids, pets and home. We walked dogs together, which was her passion. My life was hers. I lived for her and the kids. There was no restriction on anything she ever wanted.

The reality is that I think she is lost in life. Unsure of her own life goals or what happiness she seeks. She is destined to repeat the same cycles that have plagued her before. It's impossible to be happy when your desires are unknown. Jumping from relationship to relationship for the quick and immediate attention only lasts so long. Not being able to cope alone and find yourself doesn't provide any answers. Amongst this mess and chaos are Emma and Jessie. Emma is connected to Casey's family; Jessie's home is with me and mine. It's imperative that Casey's destructive behaviour doesn't become the norm for Jessie. It's my responsibility to make sure she has a stable and loving upbringing not plagued by selfish and manipulative actions.

25

NOVEMBER CONTACT

The next phone call with Jessie was again on the loudspeaker. It beggar's belief that Casey won't relinquish any control and put our daughter first. Like me, she didn't like the calls being so open and intrusive. Unable to speak freely, knowing that everyone in the room can hear our conversation. We are usually lighthearted, but when Jessie has anything on her mind, she can speak to me in confidence. At present, she is unable to open up on how she's feeling.

Saturday 4th November 2017 was our first contact session since the short visit home in half-term. A shorter time together than the upcoming meetings. Due to the limited time, there wasn't an opportunity to plan anything fun outside the city centre. I did have a few ideas for the more extended contact in a fortnight.

Shelly took four bags of clothes from me as we approached the handover location in Liverpool city centre. I wasn't permitted to attend, and Casey had left personal belongings at our family home. I didn't want to destroy her property, so I felt the urge to return stuff a bit at a time in manageable quantities. While I have the car, Casey is restricted to travelling via public transport. Over-exerting her wouldn't be of any benefit.

Witnessing Casey walking away was my cue to approach Jessie at the earliest opportunity. I was so eager to see her. Picking her up off the ground and enjoying an affectionate cuddle. We walked a short journey with her in my arms until I put her back down on the ground, continuing to walk holding hands.

"Does Emma have her ears pierced?" I asked

"Yes."

"Is that why you want yours done?"

"Yeah."

"Was you asking me for a phone because Emma has one?"

"Yep."

"Your too young for a phone. You don't need to have everything Emma has. She's older. Who would you call?"

"You." Jessie eagerly responded.

"You should be able to talk to me through mummy. I don't want you to be Emma. I want you to be Jessie.

"I want to be you." Jessie declared.

"Well, I want to be you," I announced.

The plan was agreed with Casey, for me to take Jessie to get her ears pierced. To my surprise, Jessie was anxious about the procedure. Previously she was confident and eager to have the piercing. Now she was scared.

"Mummy didn't want to take me to get my ears done. She can't cope when I'm upset." Jessie explained

"The lady said it doesn't hurt much."

"Emma said it hurts and that I'll cry."

"Don't listen to everything she says. They wouldn't let kids have it done if it hurt too much. You'll be fine."

"Girls at high school have their nose, eyes and tongue pierced," Jessie explained.

"See it can't be that bad."

I remained with Jessie to comfort her; I asked Shelly to get a teddy from the store shelf for Jessie to hold. I was looking for an opportunity to distract her mind so she can relax. The member of staff performing the procedure had six piercings on one ear. She showed Jessie and explained it doesn't hurt as she's had so many herself. I didn't want to pressure Jessie into doing something she doesn't want. At the same time, I didn't want fear to restrict her from doing something she was so excited for just a short time prior.

The procedure was over instantly, success. Then the scream bellowed out from such a small person. Jessie was uncontrollable. I hugged her and held her tightly.

"It's over now. It was quick. You're so brave." I said with pride.

"It hurts."

"It'll calm down soon. It's just a bit sore. You'll be fine."

One ear recovered fine; the other took around an hour for the pain to subside. She was traumatised by the experience but excited to choose earrings. It felt as though she was growing up too fast, but her selection reassured me - My Little Pony. She is not losing her youth just yet.

"You'll never have to have them done again. It's all finished."

I proceeded to give Jessie many hugs and kisses. I felt terrible that she had suffered. I'd never had any piercings in my life. I had trusted the advice of the staff. I think the negative remarks Emma had ingrained into Jessie's mind made her anxious and expected pain. As soon as she felt the needle touch her skin, it was enough for her to feel frightened.

Shelly needed to look at some clothes in nearby shops. She went on her own as Jessie was in no mood to browse at this moment. I know Jessie better than anyone. I could see that something else was bothering her beyond the pain of having her ears pierced.

"What's bothering you," I asked

"Nothing."

"I know something's bothering you."

"Mummy said, I couldn't tell you."

"I can't know what school you go to or where you live, but we can talk about anything else."

"Mummy said I couldn't talk about him."

"Who?" I curiously asked.

"Mummy said that you'd say Connor is a stranger, but we've known him since we arrived in Liverpool."

"Well. He's a stranger to me as I don't know him, but if you feel safe around him, then I'm okay with it. You can talk about him. It doesn't upset me.

"I asked Mummy if she is marrying Connor, but she said no, they're just friends."

A weight had been lifted from Jessie's mind. A secret she was having to hold in and keep from me released with no bad feelings. It was a relief for her. For me, it explained a lot. Up to now, most of the circumstances hadn't made sense. Why Casey left so abruptly? The heartless behaviour. The list goes on. My family and solicitors were confident from the start that Casey was most likely in a relationship. Connor looks to be the reason for her decisions.

We headed to The Harvester for lunch with Shelly accompanying us after her shopping excursion. This helped completely take Jessie's mind from her ear. The focus was now me. She'd pretend to kiss my cheeks though instead licking them. Just one of the many pranks we play on each other. My "Eww" response had her in fits of laughter.

I said to Jessie "Trust no-one." Then motioned for her to come closer. "Come here. You know you can trust me."

Jessie hesitated "You just said, trust no-one." She knew that I was being sneaky and not to trust me as it's almost certain that I will do something to her.

Eventually, I got within range of Jessie and blew raspberries on her cheek. It had us both laughing. I had my revenge for the lick she did to me. Jessie then joined me at the salad bar to get a few small snacks to eat. She's rather wild without any care of who's nearby — jumping on me with incredible enthusiasm. We played together, forgetting our surroundings and where we were. For that moment, we transcended from the reality of our environment. I gave her plenty of kisses and cuddles while also licking her cheek and blowing raspberries.

"Do you do this with mummy?" I asked.

"No mummy would tell me off. She isn't silly like us." Jessie responded.

Jessie unexpectedly remarked upon someone visiting her and showed photos of my home.

"Where did she meet you?"

"At school."

It was evident by Jessie's expression that I knew of the person she was referring. I didn't want to give anything away that she isn't supposed to know, so I tried to get her to lead the conversation.

"Was this person white?" I asked

"Nope"

"What's her name?"

"I can't remember. You tell me." Jessie suggested with a mischievous smile.

"Let me think. Was it - Jasmin?"

"Yep."

"I've already spoken to her."

"She also came to our home and saw Emma's bed. It was a mess and not even made."

Jessie switched her attention to Shelly, "Are you helping my daddy."

"Yep," Shelly responded proudly.

"Shelly takes time out of her life from her family to help me."

"It's worth it for a very special little girl." Shelly acknowledged.

"Ahh". Jessie responded with a smile.

We ordered our meals and Jessie resumed her harassment by jumping all over me.

"How's Emma getting on with school?" I enquired.

"Since she started high school, she's had an attitude. Doesn't do homework and always has detention."

"Does mummy help with the homework?"

"Mummy can't do anything. She can't even do 100x100."

"What is it then?" I asked

"One hundred." She responded with confidence.

"No, it's not."

"Yes, it is." Looking at me as though I'm stupid.

"No. 100x1 is one hundred."

"Oh yeah, that's it."

"The answer is 10,000. You do 1x1. Then you add all the 0's together. So, you get 10,000."

"When Emma came back to Chelmsford, she wanted to play with her old school friends. They knew she was down but wouldn't respond to her messages until after she returned to Liverpool."

"Does she speak to her dad?"

"No, not really."

I felt sad for Emma as I always did things with both Jessie and her. She was never left out. Emma isn't happy or settled. She had been dedicated to school, priding herself on doing well and handing in homework. Of course, kids do change at high school. The difference was startling in such a short space of time.

"I've done a Christmas hamper of treats for Emma." I leaned over to Jessie to show her the photo on my phone "She can't know as it's a present."

"Ahh. I'll give it for you." Jessie responded with a smile.

"It's too heavy."

"I'll tell Emma that you do care about her."

Arriving at the Disney store switched both of our attention away from the circumstances we have to endure. Jessie wanted more toys than I had anticipated. She loved all of the Moana items along with everything in-between. A jewellery box had her intrigued. It was ideal for her new earrings, so I purchased that for her.

The Entertainer shop provided Jessie with more opportunities to point out all the toys she wants for Christmas. I was struggling to keep up and mentally document everything she listed. A few items were on sale, so I purchased a Nerf crossbow for less than £10 for her to take back to her mother's home. Hatchimals were the big thing this year for Christmas. I'd never heard of them. In our time apart, I had lost touch of what toys are all the rage. As tends to be the case with popular kids toys, these Hatchimals don't come cheap — each around £70 and like the now less fashionable Furby. The trouble is the toy is a random secret. There's no knowing what colour or model is inside.

Our final purchases were in WH Smith. I bought three Diary of the Wimpy Kid books. Two for Jessie and one for me. They were on a promotional deal. Jessie and I have a copy of the same book so she can read to me during our telephone calls.

Jessie, Shelly and I concluded the day by heading to a coffee shop. Much to her delight, Jessie had a hot chocolate drink and a large cookie. She would jump on me and be rather silly in-between each sip of her drink. We enjoyed ourselves. It didn't matter where we were or what we are doing. The only important thing is being together. Both of us had smiles on our faces enjoying every moment and embracing every opportunity to play and be affectionate. The separation has been incredibly hard on us both.

As we left the coffee shop, Shelly made a playful remark. Jessie wasn't impressed. "That's my dad you are talking about!" She exclaimed.

Jessie's fiercely protective of me in the same way that I am towards her.

She kept waving back at me as she walked back to Casey. Even while in her care, Jessie continued to wave in my direction. Shelly told me after that Casey had waived to me too; however, I hadn't noticed. I was too transfixed and focused on Jessie to see anything else. I did; however, notice Casey change direction walking towards me behind Shelly. She was oblivious to what was going on. Fearing a clash between us, I walked away from the area to reduce any chance of conflict.

The 8th November 2017 phone call was later than expected. Casey sent me a text message informing of her delay due to the bus stuck in traffic. I didn't mind and appreciated the update. The phone rang at 6.45pm. I could hear Jessie's voice.

"Who is this?" I asked.

Jessie could be heard laughing. She knew I was messing about knowing full well that it's her on the line as expected.

"Did you hear. Daddy, did you hear?"

"Hear what? Did I hear what? - about grandad?"

"Yeah," Jessie responded.

"I do know. I agreed that mummy would be the one to tell you. Grandad loved you and Emma, and he knows that you loved him too." I assured her. "You managed to give him a hug."

"Oakley wouldn't even cuddle him or have his photo taken!" Jessie explained

"He was just excited and wanted to play with you."

"Yeah, he did." Jessie acknowledged.

The conversation soon shifted to what we would be doing next weekend. Jessie had assumed that she would be seeing me in Chelmsford. I corrected her by explaining it's in-fact taking place in Liverpool for the following few contacts.

"I'm still learning the area, but I know it's important for you that we be able to talk. As we have longer together, we may be able to travel a bit in the car." I explained, "If we go in the car, we have to make sure we're back in time and make sure we don't get stuck in traffic."

"OK. I've been having fun with the Nerf gun you bought me. I shoot it at a dartboard."

"That's good. Just to let you know you can tighten the earrings after the first night."

"I want to keep them loose until the six weeks has finished."

"It's up to you. I've bought you and Emma advent calendars. That's if she wants it."

"Yay. I already have one, so now I'll have two. Could use one for November." Jessie responded with excitement.

"I can eat one of them for you. If it helps, I could take a before and after photo before I eat it. Would that be good?" I cheekily suggested.

"No, it wouldn't. I want it." Responding with authority.

She knew that I was joking but didn't want me misinterpreting the desire to eat it herself.

"I've been filling your hamper with treats. I'll give you three guesses of the chocolate I bought which you love." I revealed.

"Dairy Milk."

"Nope."

After using all of her guesses, she failed miserably. Considering she was suggesting her favourite chocolates, maybe it was I that failed.

"Ferrero Rocher" I revealed.

"Ooh. I forgot about that."

"I've been struggling not to eat it. So, tempting."

"You would, wouldn't you."

"I wouldn't eat anything of yours silly."

Jessie laughed, "Yes, you would."

Reading was now at the forefront of our minds. I told Jessie that if she can't decide which book then close her eyes and point to one. The first page read "For Dad."

"Oh, that's for me, give it to me. It's mine." I demanded.

I could hear Jessie laughing. She often finds my behaviour whimsical and funny. Jessie went on to read four pages from one of the Diary of a Wimpy Kid books. Her reading was impressive and had improved significantly since she last read to me. Longer words were a struggle though such as 'exhausted'. I did my best to support her with the correct pronunciation when she struggled. Some words were harder than others to assist as I didn't have a pen and paper to read back the spelling. I commented that I would get more books so that I can follow along with her.

Hearing Jessie read was another milestone in my pursuit to get back to the life we had before the chaos. Even though we aren't together, it means the world to me that we're able to do normal everyday things regardless of the distance that separates us.

"Mummy said I have to hang up now."

"OK. Love you."

"I don't want to hang up. I love you." Jessie pleaded.

"I love you too, but you need to hang up as we're using mummies credit."

"Bye, love you," Jessie responded.

Our conversation lasted thirty minutes.

26

FUNERAL

My stepdad's funeral is either side of the regularly scheduled contacts. It was an emotional event which affected the entire family. Those that were able to attend were there along with people that were part of his life that most of us had never known. He was more popular than just a family man.

I rode in the leading car with my brothers and sisters. The mood was sombre. While all of us are parents ourselves, we certainly didn't expect to be saying goodbye to one of ours so early in our lives. Our ages ranged from 34 to 42. A close-knit group though with all families, there can be some friction between one or two people. It was a day for us all to come together and we sure did.

Carrying the coffin was too much for me. I had left it undecided until we arrived. There was too much emotion, and I wasn't confident that I'd be able to hold myself together with the responsibility of carrying the coffin. Someone else took my place. Watching it brought into the hall was surreal. Inside that ornate box was my stepdad. The man that raised me as his own alongside my mother. Always treating me the same as his natural sons. There, for all of us with words of wisdom. He never failed to be there for us in our moments of need.

Holding the booklet with photos of him when he was healthy and robust was too much to bear. I was consumed in tears struggling to maintain myself, trying my best to be composed though failing every-time. The loss was profound. He will never be with us anymore. Losing him hurt the entire family. Even the children felt immense sadness. The figurehead of our lives was now receiving his farewell — no more suffering. Cancer can be cruel, and it was indeed relentless.

He had been there for all of us during our lives. For his final moments, we were all there for him. Helping him get around the home when his own body couldn't. It was painful to witness, and I'm sure even harder for him to endure. Life is just so precious. It's the love we embrace along the way that makes every moment worth living.

Being with everyone during this emotional and sad moment was somewhat therapeutic. We were all experiencing the same grief and enduring the loss. Memories were shared and often humorous moments recalled, which changed the mood to a more happy and joyful experience. My stepdad wouldn't have wanted us to spend the day sad and depressed. Enjoying our lives and continuing to live on is how he would've wanted it. That's the best way to show our respect.

I had a good time with the family and shared a lot of laughs. When a few of us get together, the situation can get rather silly with many pranks and jokes. All of us together and it's a riot. There were plenty of laughs.

The food at the wake hadn't been the best quality. Considering the expense, it should've been much better. I felt rather daring. Along with two others, we went up to the serving area and helped ourselves to a carvery. It should've been the food option in the first place. In all honesty, I was beginning to lose the plot, contending with the biggest battle of my life. Fighting for Jessie was never far from my mind. Now I've lost one of my role-models and a large part of my support system. Even if Jessie can come home one day, the life she returns to will never be the same.

I left the venue before everyone else. Said my goodbyes and walked my way back to mums' home. It was only a short walk, which provided time to collect my thoughts. I drove my car off the driveway and made my way home. Recently the problem for me, when surrounded by people, is that I become uncomfortable after a period. Unable to shake off the feeling that Jessie is missing. So much time apart causes me to lose myself and struggle to find happiness in any moments when she's not with me.

27

CONFUSION

By now, a few contact sessions had passed. Jessie and I were having the time of our lives. We did various activities, including bowling and enjoyed a meal at a restaurant. We also had others in attendance, whether it be Shelly or my mum. Something of a life together was beginning to take shape. At least the best we can do for now considering the distance and inability to bring her home just yet. It beat mindlessly walking around the same row of shops repeatedly.

When the report finally arrived, I was left bemused by its contents. It was apparent to me that Casey had manipulated the findings and lied her way through the session with the psychiatrist. Even he questioned her honesty regarding how long she suffered from depression. By her accounts, it's recent and that Emma's dad and I are the cause. The psychiatrist noted that previous therapy reports disclosed that Casey had previously mentioned suffering with mental health as a child. Her problems stemmed from the lack of attention she received from her parents. Post-natal depression from both pregnancies made her condition more severe as it had not been treated.

The original psychiatrist report hadn't encompassed Casey's GP history as the records hadn't been received.

Everyone was now waiting on an updated addendum from the psychiatrist, which will explain his findings of those records. It is due imminently and then Casey and I are to provide statements in response. Our accounts were attributable in November, but the report has suffered delays. Without it, we would have nothing to respond to, so we were bound by the report. My solicitors frantically tried to find a solution as it seemed everyone was falling apart. Casey's solicitors hadn't confirmed whether they had received her requested GP reports. Without them, the psychiatrist couldn't file his addendum·report which in-turn made it impossible for CAFCASS to file the S7 report. It seemed as if we were the only ones left out of the loop, not knowing what everyone is doing. Until everyone else has their houses in order we can't do anything.

The biggest problem is that the current order only specifies contact up to the 2nd of December. It is expected that we would attend court to arrange future contact along with the S7 report and psychiatrist addendum. If Casey and I can agree on a schedule of contact up to the new year, then the upcoming court hearing can be cancelled until all the reports are available.

Casey refused to engage and accept my reasonable contact terms. I proposed that I would have Jessie fortnightly weekends. I collect her from Liverpool on the Fridays while Casey travels to Chelmsford to collect on the Sundays. The judge was never going to adjourn a hearing without any agreement in place. We were desperate for the hearing to go ahead as Casey wasn't responding.

It was frustrating arriving at the short court hearing. The only thing that was on the agenda was a new timetable for submissions and agreeing on a contact schedule. Casey was now open to discussions. It's ridiculous that she has made me travel the length of the country and incur legal fees close to one thousand pounds when she could've engaged with me sooner. Every single hearing is costly. There's no such thing as a cheap court hearing.

As Casey is publicly funded, she's not liable for any costs. It's for this reason that she has no problem making me attend court hearings which are almost irrelevant. While my solicitors are acting for me for free, I am still responsible for paying the barrister's who represent me in court. The costs are mounting and its money that could be better spent on improving Jessie's life.

In the courtroom District Judge Thomas was bemused. Casey was pleading poverty. Her stance was that she couldn't contribute anything to the travels costs nor travel to Chelmsford. Casey explained through her barrister that she must care for Emma, and it wouldn't be appropriate for her to travel so far and back again. She never bothered to respond at all to my request for contact proposals before court. It was difficult to understand why there was no counter offer to my proposals with this information. Instead, she had just been ignorant, keeping her reasons secret to surprise me in court at a significant financial cost to me.

I was so close to laughing. Casey always plays the victim somehow. Now she's the victim of finances. I travel up and down the country. My financial situation is worse than hers. My mum is supporting me throughout these proceedings. Casey's father owns a boat of reasonable value. She decided to move so far away so she should bear the responsibility of that decision and the logistics involved. It shouldn't be for me to be burdened with everything when I've done absolutely nothing wrong. As my mum supports me, I couldn't understand why her family couldn't help her. It seems as though some people have different priorities in life. Jessie means more to us than she does to them.

With her finances in such disarray, the judge was almost powerless to enforce her to contribute now. He did, however, warn her "Your client needs to budget her finances by the next hearing as she will most certainly be contributing towards the travel."

For now, we are bound to spend our contacts in Liverpool. It's not what I had proposed or wanted, but I am bringing her home for a few days after Christmas for the festive period. Hopefully the start of many more times at home.

While stuck in Liverpool we had a good time. My niece Clarissa joined us on the travel north to stay in a hotel with Jessie, mum and I for the weekend. We went swimming and watched the movie 'Wonder' at the cinema. It was a great movie which Jessie enjoyed. She is such a compassionate child and felt sad for the boy that he was treated so bad by others. Thankfully by the end of the movie, it was rather uplifting.

In the hotel, we played board games, many pranks and generally plenty of laughs. As always, the days fly by, and

Jessie's anxiety increases. She worries that our time is coming to an end. I always reassure her that in any event we will speak regularly and see each other soon.

During one of our conversations, it transpired that Casey's sister Becky hadn't been to visit, in all the time that they had been in Liverpool. I was shocked. Their relationship had always been close. Becky would often stay at our home regularly and loved spending time with the children. She became busier when she got into the relationship that she remains into this day. I couldn't comprehend that neither of them had made any effort to see each other. They live far apart, but it's not impossible. I travel their regularly, often only for short visits, and then I drive home.

Something isn't right. I didn't want Jessie to suffer due to their lack of commitment in seeing each other or potential argument they may be having. Becky always - and I do mean *always* visited the kids on their birthday or the day after depending on our plans. I have a lot of respect for her with regards to the kids. My battle with Casey, and by extension, her parents don't extend to her sister. She may harbour ill feelings towards me due to any manipulation by Casey or her mother. It's not about me, though. I only care about what's best for Jessie.

I sent Becky a message via Facebook asking whether she would like to spend time with Jessie while in my care over the Christmas period.

ME: Hi Becky, Jessie's been home for a few days. She goes back to Liverpool tomorrow. I'm taking her swimming today. I've always respected the efforts you go to for the kids so if you would like to see Jessie, I'm happy for you to see her. I did suggest you could take her for a short while, but she doesn't want to be apart from me so your welcome to visit her at my mums' home this evening. I can free up the kitchen for you to spend time with her to save any awkwardness you may feel. It's comfy with stalls. I asked Jessie if she's seen you since she left, and I was surprised she hadn't so felt it would be nice for her to see you. If you're busy it's not a problem.

BECKY: Hi thank you for thinking of me very nice of you! I could drop by with Jessie's presents come in to say hi and give her gifts, but would it be ok if John came too if not I understand?

ME: Yeah there's no problem he's welcome to come with you. I'll message you when I'm at my mums then you can pop round whenever is convenient for you.

She was eager to spend time with Jessie. Becky missed their time together. It's not only my family and me that have suffered throughout all of this but other people too. All of us are innocent victims of Casey's actions.

I had only anticipated Becky visiting Jessie for a short while. She became so comfortable that she stayed for an hour or two. At first, I left them alone to give them privacy and quality time together. Jessie kept running out randomly to provide me with a cuddle in the kitchen. She had a great time with Becky and John. Eventually, they joined us in the kitchen and shared many laughs. Jessie enjoyed the attention. It was a perfect day, memorable and absolutely the correct decision to make happen.

Shortly after she left, Becky sent me a lovely message mentioning that she had had fun.

BECKY: Thank you for this evening! Was lovely seeing Jessie

ME: No problem she loved it. I have her in 2 weeks, but time is limited. When I have her longer again, I'll let you know so you can spend time with her. I only ever want her to be happy, she had a great time

BECKY: Ok cool thank you

Some presents from Casey's family had been left with me to bring along to the handover when I return Jessie. Upon returning her, Casey appeared surprised at receiving the bags full of gifts. As some were from her mother, I had anticipated that she would've at least informed Casey in advance of my arrival.

My solicitors received correspondence from Casey's early into the new year when the solicitors re-opened from the Christmas period. Casey was outraged that I had made arrangements with her sister without her involvement. She felt that it was inappropriate for me to be contacting her family directly. I was astounded. Casey has a history of being ignorant and taking weeks to respond to anything. That is no exaggeration. She needs to be prompted regularly to answer simple questions. The plan for Jessie to spend time with her auntie was a spur of the moment decision. There wasn't time to involve Casey.

It was risky for me to contact her sister personally. I knew that it could be twisted and used against me somehow in court. She always seems to find a way of turning everything. I still did it anyway. I'll answer to any potential accusations if required. The only thing that mattered was Jessie getting to spend time with more of her family.

In Liverpool, Jessie is isolated with just her mother and sister. The same faces every day, and Connor's family for support. It annoyed me no end knowing that he and his family spend so much time with Jessie while those that have been part of her life from the beginning have to clutch at small random moments of opportunity. Certainly not justified. Jessie deserves so much better. I'm trying to repair the damage in her life.

28

THE NEW YEAR

The journeys have been long and arduous. Driving a round trip of five hundred miles isn't accessible by a long shot. Some days are harder than others. It's exhausting having to suffer through the darkness on those late nights along the isolating roads. An alternative travel option had become apparent. Direct flights from Stansted airport to Liverpool could be an option. Rather than drive for around five hours, the journey would be less than an hour. Of course, there are waiting times to consider and the risk of delays. The same applies to traffic on the roads. Always unpredictable. No two journeys are ever the same. It would certainly be easier on me and much less tiresome for Jessie. We'd have more quality time together even if it's waiting at the airport. Better than being glued to a steering wheel. She's always wanted to experience flying. It could be the perfect opportunity — something for me to investigate anyway. I needed to figure out the logistics and arrival times.

The city of Liverpool is new to me. I do my best with the help of the map feature on my phone. Public transport, though, would be a step too far from my comfort and knowledge. After much research and diligence, I suggested to Casey via my legal representatives.

Were either of us to travel by plane then the other parent should be met at the airport for the handover.

It's much more practical than have the flying parent then need to seek further transport after the journey. We both benefit as it's a valid option for us. Casey travels via train, but the comparable costs are negligible, and the trip is so much quicker. I would meet her at Stansted, and she meets me at Liverpool.

I received confirmation that Casey agreed to my suggestion. It could be the way forward for us. Air travel bridges the distance and makes the transition between our lives and the location much more manageable. Jessie would feel much closer to home and not a world apart.

As the upcoming court date drew nearer, there was a concern that the CAFCASS S7 report was still overdue. There had been so many delays, and I'd provided a vast amount of information to the officer in question. I was looking forward to the report. Word soon spread that the report won't be submitted in time for the court hearing. I was in shock. They have had months to investigate, talk to all parties and assess all the evidence and various reports. What could the reason be for not submitting the report yet again?

The official stance was that the officer in question became ill and unable to finish the report. I didn't believe this response at all because she was so close to a decision. I had spoken to her on the telephone only a week or two prior.

She was aware of everything that had been going on between Casey and me. She told me personally that she was just finalising her report. There was no indication of what way her decision was leaning. I do know, though that she was frustrated by Casey's lack of engagement. Very difficult to get any responses to questions she doesn't like. Always hiding the truth and being secretive.

I think Jasmin was removed from the case by a supervisor or someone above her. That's my opinion, and I can't justify any reasoning that they may have. Maybe her report wasn't strong enough, or there were errors. All I could see was incompetence from CAFCASS. Simple tasks were becoming too much for them. I don't like to criticise, but they haven't been the most professional at times. Some officers, especially those early on, were brilliant. They seem to rotate every-time. Not having continuity didn't make any sense.

So now we still have a court date looming. So much uncertainty about how long the court process is going to take, in light of the missing S7 report. I'd expect the judge to be somewhat perplexed and fuming at the further delays. It's evident to me that he does place children at the forefront of proceedings. Putting Jessie into prolonged turmoil isn't in her best interests. She's being failed miserably by the authorities.

I'm available at any notice and will always respond promptly to any requests. In-fact Jasmin phoned while I was driving north to visit Jessie. It wasn't the best time to be calling. I'm sure Casey had the most comfortable experience with personal visits and calls at home. I was stressed from the heavy driving and struggling to hear on the telephone from a services car park. I did my best to communicate and provide responses to Jasmin's questions.

I hated the idea of delaying anything. There have been too many delays already. Most of which is Casey's fault. She doesn't respond to anything on time and makes up so many lies to cause further disruption. I need to keep the train moving and be incredibly efficient. Imagine the chaos if we both behaved the same as Casey!

I didn't think Jasmin was the best CAFCASS officer to be assigned, but she was our point of contact. She seemed slow at times to process information and wasn't aware of much going on around her. I had to update her on dates and times etc. personally. She didn't even know that she was provided with an extension to file the report in January. With Casey and I, events happen continually. It's a minefield of change and bitterness between us. Somehow CAFCASS and the court were out of the loop regarding the most current developments. Most of our issues were dealt with solely between legal representatives. I would make the court aware of her behaviour within my statements where permitted. It can only be done when the court requests statements, which in most cases are months later than the actual events.

I did provide updates to Jasmin regularly, but some moments were missed. I must be delicate and strike a balance between being informative and not controlling. It's open to interpretation and annoying that being so open can get me into trouble. My intentions could be misinterpreted.

I prefer to be myself, open and honest, but sadly, the world doesn't always look favourably on that.

The court date went ahead without the S7 report, and no current CAFCASS officer assigned to our case. It was a mess, and the day only became more confusing. Back in December, the judge was very firm with Casey. While she was having difficulties assisting with any travel arrangements, she needed to budget herself to help in future. To my surprise and the judges, Casey was adamant that she can't commit to taking on any of the travel between Liverpool and Chelmsford.

The mess we are in and the distance between us is all her fault. She should have considered this before uprooting such a vast distance. It's not my responsibility to resolve the situation alone. The judge was furious and reminded her about the previous directions from the last court hearing. He responded that she WILL be assisting, going forward.

I didn't feel that he went far enough, but his order was that she does one travel per month. It was left open for her to choose when she would be able to travel. I didn't like that at all. Provide Casey freedom to be disruptive, and she will grab it with both hands and become a nightmare. I was certainly not optimistic.

On the one hand, she has finally been ordered to do something. On the other, she has the power to disrupt any plans I have in place. I won and lost at the same time. She was less smug though at that moment, so that was a positive to take from the situation.

She argued that neither child's fathers are contributing financially towards their children. I almost burst out laughing. It's Casey's fault that we are sitting here in court before a judge. She is publicly funded and pays nothing towards these court hearings. My costs are in the thousands of pounds for each trial. Legal fees, fuel, hotel and meals. I still never let Jessie go without essentials. I buy her clothes, meals and snacks when she is in my care, toys and anything she needs for school. I provide for her and must endure the costs of travel and court.

Casey is sad for herself that she doesn't financially gain anything beyond her benefits. I am more than happy to have Jessie in my care and never receive any payments from her. If she didn't reside so far away, which results in excessive costs from travel, then, of course, I would contribute to her life with Casey. The journey costs far exceed any maintenance payments. I felt that it was a low blow to complain about the lack of financial assistance. More so in the fact that she didn't mention any of the money I spend on Jessie. She is not a child neglected by her father.

29

CHILD ABUSE

As always, the court can be rather stressful and frustrating. For all of the positive expectations and desire for success, it's never straightforward and always unpredictable. Court had been something of a mixed bag. The good news is that after court I will be collecting Jessie for our weekend contact. It provided a nice distraction and eased any frustrations.

The court process has been long, with no end in sight. Whenever it seems to be concluding, obstacles disrupt the process and prolong the suffering. I browsed through shops as I awaited Jessie's arrival into the city centre. She arrived with Emma and a school friend in attendance. My only focus was Jessie and making the transition as swift as possible. We have a long journey south, and I no longer desire to be in the company of Casey or Emma. The reality is that their body language and demeanour annoy me. They exude smugness and arrogance.

We travelled south with Jessie enjoying movies on the iPad. I connected the device to the car speakers so that she can have a cinema-like experience. She loves it, and the film is more immersive, thus alleviating the journey from feeling too long and draining.

When we arrived, Jessie didn't want to do anything other than soaking up the home that she adored. I offered her various options such as swimming, but she was firm in her desire to remain at home. It's sad to witness her clinging to the life that she had to leave behind with such anxiety. All I want is for her to be comfortable, happy and relaxed. She must cope with a lot. As the weekend evolved, it became apparent that her life in the care of her mother is not all that it seems. Casey portrays an image of harmony and placing the children above everything. It is certainly not the case. What Jessie told me is alarming and requires addressing.

Jessie and I have a lot of fun together. We're silly, goofy and don't take life too seriously. It's just a breeze and effortless. As she tries to transfer that light-heartedness to living up north, she's met with boredom and frustration. A simple quip to her mother "Lighten up" is received with a firm remark in response. Jessie was trying to encourage more fun and expressive mother. Completely lost on Casey. She doesn't know how to play with kids. Everything is just serious and adult.

My family and I are so like one another in that we are all rather outgoing and love to laugh. Jessie is the same, though it's in direct contrast to Casey and her family. We are just opposites. I made the point that Casey's sister Becky laughs. Jessie responded, "She should have been in our family." It made me laugh as it was so right. Without being rude to Casey and her family, she does appear to be the only one that laughs and has positivity to her personality.

Jessie explained that she had informed Casey on many occasions that she desires to live me. The response she received was shocking. Of course, I can understand a feeling of disrespect, but I would expect mature handling of the situation. Instead, Casey behaves like an immature child. "Tough luck." was the response with no opportunity for any discussion on the subject. Simply cutting Jessie off from expressing herself. It's sad to hear. I can only imagine her sadness and feeling of isolation in those moments.

When conversations turn to me, Casey becomes angry and enraged. It's a subject Jessie isn't free to discuss. In my presence, Jessie is free to talk about anyone. Even though I hate Casey for everything that she has done and continues to do to Jessie and I., My feelings are put to one side so that she is comfortable talking about her life without worry or fear of being judged. I listen and observe what she says and try my best to respond positively while remembering anything of significance.

The next thing that Jessie told me was shocking and confusing. I couldn't understand how a parent could order their child to behave in such a way. She is made to feel wrong, naughty and self-critical. The list goes on, and it's not behaviour that a child should ever witness, let alone be told to do to themselves. Casey is in denial so never responds to any criticism or concerns. In her mind, she's a saint and can do no wrong. The reality is that she is a monster, cruel and narcissistic.

Jessie has been instructed to tell herself off! I've witnessed her hit herself in frustration and call herself stupid. It's profoundly alarming and heartbreaking. In my care, she is like a butterfly. So positive and free to express herself. Her world away from me is shocking and dark. Authorities turn a blind eye and swayed by Casey's denials. It was only later that I saw Jessie hit herself. If she had done it around this time, then I would've pressed the matter more strongly and not relented. It is not acceptable and disgusting. Casey should be ashamed of herself.

Rather than keep adult issues to herself, she has publicly accused me of abuse to her family and friends even in Jessie's presence. It upsets Jessie deeply. She knows my character and that it's not true. She shouldn't be subjected to such conversations. It's abhorrent to label someone with such an accusation when it's so far from the truth. I've never cared what people think of me, but Jessie does. I know myself and proud of who I am. I stand up for my family and will always be honourable. Supported Casey throughout all of her mental health issues and took care of all responsibility of the kids.

I'm hardly going to waste my time convincing Casey of everything I did. If it helps her to view my actions in a different light, then that's for her to come to terms with in the future. The damage has already been done. I will never forgive her. It does cross my mind from time to time to take the accusations further and subject her to proceedings for slander. For now, I bide my time and focus solely on Jessie. She always comes first. I would hope that the accusations eventually stop so that life can move forward freely. If not, then I will have no choice but to address it head on which will be of immense embarrassment to Casey. Her lies are profound and will look foolish in-time.

Casey has ordered Jessie not to cry upon her return from our contacts. Of course, it's not nice to witness, but Jessie should be free to express her emotions. Holding it in will only cause her issues in future. It's preferable that as parent's we comfort her and listen to what she has to say. Only then will she become more comfortable and possibly content with the current situation. Denying her the simple act of feeling sad is somewhat controlling and negative. While I encourage Jessie to express herself, Casey demands that she doesn't. It's not conducive of positive parenting.

There's a lack of freedom in her life when venturing between households. I'm happy for Jessie to bring anything she likes to our home and it can be returned when we go back. Anything that comes from my house will never be seen again. It's lost up north and mysteriously ends up going missing no matter how hard Jessie tries to find a place to stow safely. It's absolute madness. I don't know what goes through Casey's mind, but it's exhausting dealing with her. The look of fear on Jessie's face when she contemplates whether to take anything back with her is sad. She shouldn't have to worry as she does. She deserves to be happy.

School meals are something of an issue. It's a severe problem. Jessie is a very selective eater. Incredibly picky and difficult to feed beyond her preferred choices. She does need to try different foods.

Schools seem to vary on how they provide meals. At Jessie's school, it is facilitated by a phone app. The parent selects the food choice for each school day. It does seem open to abuse with no real monitoring. I say this because Casey opts for the same meals every day and food that she knows Jessie hates. Jacket potatoes and sometimes pizza. There are meal options that she would like, but Casey won't select them, and there's nothing Jessie can do to override the choices made by her mother. It's disturbing. I'm witnessing so much abuse of my daughter in so many ways by Casey and no-one is reacting or helping Jessie. How can she be fed the same meals every day? And then when she goes home, it's the same thing for dinner. Hardly ever gets provided a side dish of beans, vegetables or salad. It requires too much effort.

Participates in extra-curricular school clubs which Casey knows she hates. Jessie doesn't want to take part in a book club, but she's forced into it by her mother. There are clubs that she would love to do, such as dance but must endure being subjected to whatever Casey decides.

Casey is somewhat controlling and manipulative. Jessie overheard a telephone conversation that she was having with Connor. It's rude for Jessie to have a favourite person in her life. The fact that I'm her favourite is wrong, and if she must have a preference, it should be her. It just shows how Casey's world revolves around herself.

I wouldn't care who's Jessie's favourite. It's easy for me to say, of course when I am, but there are days when she adores other people. I don't take it personally. If she is happy, that's all that matters. That's the truth. Casey does need to look in the mirror and be honest with herself. She lives in a bubble filled with lies and deceit. Jessie has always been attached to me, but aside from that, it's worth analysing the behaviour of everyone. What would draw Jessie towards her mother? I struggle to find anything positive to say, and I don't even have to endure living with her. When you have someone so negative and obstructive in your life, it's hardly surprising that you would want to get away from them.

It messes with Jessie's mind when she is falsely accused of being unappreciative upon receiving gifts. She's the most thoughtful and kind child I have ever met. I don't say this because she's my daughter. It's an observation. She is very well mannered and is always appreciative. I find it abusive to play with her emotions in such a way. Causing her to self-doubt and lose her self-esteem. If we're going to point at anyone, it's Emma that is far from polite. She is never thankful and expects the world. Jessie has told me many stories, and it appears as though Emma hasn't improved at all with age. Either Casey is taking Emma's behaviour out on Jessie, or she's punishing her for not being bought emotionally by gifts. Either way, it's abhorrent.

By all accounts, it's not a fun life up north. Casey and Emma never smile and are rarely happy. Jessie bears the brunt of their frustrations. Emma is cold and ignorant of her desire to play and have fun together. Casey reprimands her for innocuous things such as being disturbed when watching TV. It seems to me that she just can't fit in and do right in the life expected of Casey.

Why on earth Casey selected a school for Jessie to attend which requires waking up at 5 am is beyond me. There's no way that it's Jessie's best interest. She's exhausted by lunchtime. Her eyes are red and tired when I collect her from the strain of having to get up so early. It transpires that her school is within very close proximity to Connor's family. Jessie continues to suffer for Casey's relationship with Connor. She is dragged across the country so abruptly away from everyone that she loves into a life of exhaustion. All this so that Casey can be close to Connor. The actions of a loving mother who could never place the children above herself.

When our time gets closer to an end, Jessie becomes anxious. She doesn't want to return to Casey and the life she never wanted up north. She desires to remain with me in the life adored. I do my best to ease the suffering by reminding her that she will be back again soon. It's difficult to witness the look of despair on her face. I remain at the mercy of the court and have to adhere to its rulings.

Casey's sister Carly was rather spiteful recently at Christmas. Jessie recently informed me that she had ignored her and provided no gift while Emma was made to feel special. She was being victimised because of her love and desire to be with me. Cruelty runs through the family. They can't look beyond their frustrations and anger. On this occasion, Casey did step up and do right by Jessie. She gave money herself. It was a beautiful act of kindness. It's just frustrating that she has no consistency and doesn't address issues with the people in question. I would've stood up against their behaviour and made it clear of my disgust. Acts of cruelty shouldn't go ignored.

As we arrived in Liverpool for Jessie's return, she becomes incredibly emotional. Close to the handover location, she was anxious. Adamant that Casey is going to shout at her. I was confused. She was distraught. So why on earth would she be reprimanded?

It became clear that Casey had been absolute in her order for Jessie not to return crying. I then asked Jessie if she would like me to have a word with Casey. She nodded and said "Yes."

Casey approached, and I explained the situation. She did her usual pretending to care routine. I can see through it. Her voice changes and becomes overly sensitive and kind. It's not her at all, but I was content as she wasn't shouting at Jessie.

They did end up arguing. It was very dysfunctional.

Casey asked Jessie "Why are you worried about crying in front of me?"

Jessie explained while consumed by tears "Because you got angry and told me not to come back crying."

"No, I didn't."

"Yes, you did. Your lying. You know you said it."

"No, I didn't. Why would you say that?"

It went back and forth. Emma was also in attendance, but she was already in tears from something that must have happened before arriving. I ended up stopping the arguing between them by explaining that it isn't getting anyone anywhere. I hugged Jessie, told her I love her and that I will be back again soon. She remained in tears, but I left without a fuss as I didn't want to make the situation any more difficult for Casey to handle. I was confident that Casey would be on her best behaviour with Jessie knowing that I am aware and monitoring the situation. Especially with the court situation looming over us.

February 2018 was drama. Casey's revised psychiatrist report revealed a lie. Throughout this saga, she's decided to point the blame at me as the cause of her issues. GP reports contradicted that. Her first episodes began years before our relationship even started.

I wasn't happy with the conclusion. I'd lived through Casey's episodes, and it was shocking. The psychiatrist played down the severity but did note that she was at risk of further depressive episodes. He felt confident that she would seek help from doctors. That is wishful thinking. She tries to hide her suffering. Keeps it to herself until she becomes a danger.

Frankly, it scares the life out of me that my daughter is in her care. If I hadn't been there when I was during our relationship, there's no knowing what would've happened. The fact that she is prone to future problems is worrying. The truth is that I was already aware of this as I had included concerns within my initial court application.

Casey has softened her behaviour since I became aware of things. After the episode of Jessie crying upon her return, Casey has been kinder to her. She is also allowing Jessie to bring items from home for our contacts together. Jessie had made her aware that I knew of her controlling behaviour. It had an impact on her to have a change of attitude.

30

TRAVEL ARRANGEMENTS

The recent court hearing had ordered Casey to assist with travel once per month. She had pleaded financial problems preventing her from helping. The judge wasn't impressed, but he allowed her time to save. The expectation was that her first travel wouldn't be until the end of February as outlined within the court order.

I was shocked to hear from Jessie that Casey would be bringing her via train on 11th February 2018. In court, it was agreed that I would travel on Friday 9th February. Plans were already in place for me to visit and spend the night with Jessie at my sister Shelly's on the way home. Jessie was excited by my plans.

To continue with Casey's demands, I would lose almost two days of contact with Jessie. She had suggested that I could take her to my sisters when they've arrived. In no way is this acceptable. It would be unnecessary travel for her. Travel to the south of the country only to then must ascend half-way back up the country to Norfolk. There was no sense in that travel arrangement. Surprisingly, Casey could miraculously buy train tickets less than two weeks after court. She had pleaded for financial hardship.

My solicitors sent a letter to Casey's representatives as a matter of urgency. They revealed our despair at the situation and re-affirmed that I will be collecting Jessie on the 9th February as previously agreed. Casey drives me crazy with her last-minute changes and demanding behaviour. She didn't even have the decency to update me. I only found out through Jessie. I knew that she would become a problem. Life isn't comfortable with her, though I always expect the worst and she certainly doesn't disappoint in that regard.

While Casey always tries to twist her disruption as a way of helping it's not lost on me what she is doing. The travel that she is demanding is for the half-term holidays. The gap in travel is much more friendly than the problematic weekends. She was trying to leave me with the grinding weekend journeys.

I make the point to my legal team that it's not acceptable for Casey to make last minute changes to travel arrangements. The travel is hard enough to arrange as it is. Ruining those plans causes so much hassle and disruption.

Casey dared to purchase non-refundable train tickets. I'm sure that this was done whilst I was contesting her travel. My solicitors had left me to decide what our stance would be. Should we make a stand and be firm? Or allow Casey to travel on this occasion.

My response was robust, "I think we should take a firm approach and adhere to the court order. The court hearing cost £1000 because Casey wouldn't commit to travel. Now all of a sudden, she's changing the terms of that order. That court order cost a lot of money. Maybe her losing her own money will make her realise that herself.

A persuasive letter was produced in response to my request. We made it clear that it wasn't for Casey to purchase train tickets for that date or to even travel. Also stated that the recent court hearing came at a substantial cost, which a large part was dealing with travel arrangements. Unacceptable for her to unilaterally suddenly decide that she will bring Jessie and demand her father does the handover. Again, it was reaffirmed that I would be travelling on the previously agreed date.

Casey pleaded for compassion and tried to twist the purchasing of tickets as a means for her to help alleviate me from travelling near my birthday. Her reasons didn't sway me, but I had achieved what I set out to make. I couldn't change the fact that she had already purchased tickets without prior agreement. She will think twice next time though which is the best I could get out of the situation.

I agreed to the proposals as the new plans allowed Jessie to remain with me for two extra days. Our time together means more to me than teaching Casey a lesson. We had spent my birthday arguing between legal representatives. Even on my birthday, I don't get left in peace. She had previously ignored my requests for proof of the train tickets. I would've focused on the time and date. Prudent of her really, I guess. A cunning victory but just more examples of her manipulative behaviour.

There was an acceptance that I would collect Jessie from Casey's dad; however, it was made clear that I viewed it as a step backwards. Admittedly, it's in Jessie's best interests to witness her parent's getting along. We also addressed the demand for me to stay clear of Emma and have the handover with the father. Throughout the past year, I have had to contend with false accusations of abuse which have not been proven. Since then, there have been multiple occasions whereby Casey and Emma have been near me without any cause for concern. It's difficult to accept the reasons for Casey to alter the arrangements. They like to play the victim for Casey's families benefit and the court. I'm sure she's told her family so many lies which she has to maintain. I don't think her dad would have approved of her actions if he knew the truth.

There was also a request for me to park my car elsewhere. I declined. Previous collections at the train stations have been excellent. I knew that her dad didn't want to park near me, but on the other side of the station doesn't have free parking. If he wants to park away from me, then that's for him to do. Ordering me isn't getting them anywhere.

It was baffling that the handover had to take place at Chelmsford train station. It was initially indicated back in October as a place to meet as it was convenient for Emma's father. At the time, I felt it unfair. He doesn't visit Emma or do any travel. I drive up and down the country. When Casey travels, I still need to drive 30 minutes by car to a train station that's not even nearby. All of this, so that his life can be easy. It's disgraceful. Casey twisted the situation as being more comfortable for her to deal with both fathers. Heaven forbid my life could be easy for once!

On this occasion, Emma wasn't even planning to spend time with her father. The holidays were to be spent with grandparents and friends from her previous school. They decided for everyone to gather at the train station, which was perplexing. It's unnecessary and exasperating.

As talks were concluding, we asked when Casey would like to have a telephone call with Jessie during the half-term holidays. Our enquiries were ignored. There was no court order in place for telephone calls between Jessie and her mother. I was just trying to provide an opportunity for them to speak while apart. After a while, without any response, we followed up with another letter. We assumed that the mother doesn't wish to have telephone contact with Jessie. Again, this was ignored. It was rather shocking. I don't understand why she wouldn't respond. Probably a tactical decision, but I can't figure out what's to be gained by anyone to be obstructive.

The half-term holidays arrived, and Jessie was on her way south for our holiday contact together. We were both excited. I waited at the train station in readiness for her arrival.

Her grandad accompanied Jessie into my care. He was frosty, stone-faced and seemed miserable. I decided not to communicate with him. My focus was Jessie. We gave each other a big hug. At my suggestion, she then gave her grandad a cuddle. We then made our way to the car to commence the journey home.

Upon getting into the car, Jessie made a startling claim. Just before the handover, Casey and her dad had referred to me as a dickhead in her presence. I was fuming. First, I was disgusted that they would speak so negatively of me in front of Jessie. Secondly, they don't say a word to me in person — just nonsense behind my back. I struggled to compose myself. I usually take the time to analyse situations and think before I act. This couldn't wait for me to liaise with my solicitors.

I needed to get this off my chest now. A firm text message was sent addressing the situation, what I had been told and the disgust I have for such remarks. I kept the message to the point and made it clear that there would be no further handovers between her father and I. Relations between us were deteriorating by the day. Sadly, Jessie was stuck in the middle of this fighting. I try my best to keep composed and always place Jessie first. Sometimes my emotions can get the better of me, but I will stand up for us when needed.

An issue ensued towards the end of the holiday contact. Jessie had suggested that her grandad would be collecting her from my home. It came as a shock as Casey hadn't informed me of any such arrangement. I never agreed for anyone to visit my address. I was adamant that I wouldn't deal with Casey's father anymore, as previously stated in a text message. It was reinforced by a letter from my solicitors. Casey was welcome to collect Jessie from my address or I would make her available to collect at the train station.

Casey took this as a violation of the court order. She also mentioned that Jessie had lied by stating that she is saddened that I have assumed that she has been truthful. I was shocked by her audacity and eagerness to question Jessie's integrity for her benefit. Casey also acted innocent. She is appalled that Jessie would use such language. Casey wondered where she would've heard such words, as she has never spoken like that in her presence. She deflects all of her negativity back on to me. It's laughable and so predictable.

Her legal team tried to strong arm me by saying that if I refuse to return Jessie, then an urgent court hearing would need to be requested. My stance was that I am fully prepared to return Jessie into her mother's care, but I'm not dealing with the father. If she is present, then I will return her as directed within the court order. They were twisting my words to work in their client's favour.

I was advised to relent on this occasion by my solicitor, as time was precious and quickly elapsing. The backlash and costs of returning to court wouldn't be worth the trouble. It's better to get this handover completed amicably and then focus on arrangements going forward. As always, I listen and adhere to my counsel. I know that they still have my best interests at heart and are equally frustrated as I.

Nothing is ever straightforward with Casey. She may say one thing at a given moment, but it soon changes. To make the weekend travel for contact at the end of February quicker I booked a flight for Jessie, my nephew David and I. There was already an agreement between both parties that we would accommodate air travel. There was no time to liaise with Casey before purchasing tickets. Costs would increase at any moment as availability reduces. She is just too slow to respond and always ignorant. Dates and times of travel remained the same. It was only the location point for the handover that would need slight alteration.

Casey reneged on our previous agreement. She now refuses to meet me at the airport. From where she resides, it wouldn't be much effort for her. I knew roughly where she lived, though I wasn't allowed to know. Jessie kept trying to reveal information to me even against my dismissals. I didn't understand the transport network, so it's more daunting for me to navigate.

The flights were booked and can't be cancelled. I was already committed to flying and had informed Jessie during a phone call which Casey would've been aware. She was excited and looking forward to the first flight in her life. I was shocked by Casey's stance. She knew that I have proof of her acceptance unless she forgets everything like Dory from Finding Nemo. How can I be expected to make travel arrangements in advance, which works out cheaper when she creates so much uncertainty?

It's frustrating that we had recently had a court hearing. As it was agreed between both parties prior, we didn't feel the need to bother the judge with the logistics. Had I known that Casey would betray the agreement, I would've suggested to the judge to include it within an order. The next court hearing isn't until Easter. There's nothing I can do to enforce handovers taking place at the airport. It is baffling and just typical of her behaviour throughout. None of us should have been shocked. Maybe we just dropped our guard thinking she's going to be more reasonable going forward. I've learnt never to trust her, no matter how nice and fair she may seem at times. The devil hides in many disguises.

Now I had to investigate the times and routes for a train after we've landed. It would become a real situation of planes, trains and automobiles. I am driving to the airport, flying to Liverpool and then travelling by rail to the city centre. Then do it in reverse to get home. Casey must get a bus. She's lovely like that. Heaven forbid she would need to exert some effort into making other people's lives easier.

My frustrations were relayed to Casey between solicitors. My legal representatives were equally perplexed and shocked at Casey's stance. I had warned them from the start that she is unpredictable and will be difficult at every opportunity. Throughout this saga, they have witnessed it first-hand themselves. They no longer need me to detail what we are up against, an evil individual with not an ounce of compassion or desire to help in any way and make my life difficult, and by extension, Jessie's too. She makes it very difficult to rebuild trust or anything of a positive relationship. My disdain for her grows with each proceeding day. Time and again, she never fails to do something harmful.

31

FLIGHTS

Flying was a new experience for Jessie. She was filled with excitement and intrigue. Most of her school friends had already experienced the wonder of being in an aeroplane. Some of them had over exaggerated the phenomenon of enduring the discomfort of ears popping. Jessie was told that it hurts, which did make her anxious. Her emotions were conflicting. She was excited and scared. I put her mind at ease by explaining that it doesn't hurt at all. Becomes a little bit uncomfortable but she'll be fine.

For a child, an airport is a busy and large building. There are various stages to go through to reach the lobby to await the departure. She enjoyed herself and embraced everything. Armed police were in attendance due to recent terrorist incidents. It didn't faze her, and thankfully she hadn't been aware of the current problems. I explained that they are there to keep us safe.

Her calmness was typified by being so comfortable within the surroundings that she decided to use her drink bottle to do to the current crazed bottle flip challenge. After many attempts, she finally landed the perfect bottle flip. I captured the moment on camera, which was a fantastic achievement for us to look back on.

Waiting for the flight to allow boarding became longer and more tedious than expected. We had navigated through security and enjoyed a KFC meal in the lounge area. After some jokes and games, it dawned us that there was still an hour or so before we can depart. Jessie enjoyed the added company of David accompanying us. We were relaxed and ready now for our journey home. Unfortunately, the flight wasn't prepared for us yet. David and I had already endured a trip today and travelled into the city via train. We were now in reverse almost rewinding time, retracing our footsteps as we head home with Jessie in tow.

Jessie became more excited as the clock counted closer to our departure. We had to listen intently for any announcements. When our flight was declared, we made our way with haste across the terminal. We had been waiting at the wrong gate. We needed to run across to the other side through the lounge and shops. It just made the experience more exciting for Jessie.

When we arrived through security earlier, Jessie had her photo captured for identity purposes. As we reached the final security checkpoint to reach our gate, her identity was again verified. We passed through with ease and again found ourselves waiting in yet another lobby. Although our flight had been announced, it wasn't however ready for boarding. Jessie was confused and anxious to get on board. She couldn't understand why we had to wait.

Boarding the flight was an excellent experience for Jessie. She was taking everything in from the window view to the seat tray. This wasn't an experience she would ever forget.

We won't know if it's something that she wants to do again until we lift off and find ourselves high in the sky. There is a fear inside of me that she may be hysterical. For all parents, there's an unknown of how a child will react in situations which may or may not scare them. I'm ready to comfort her and help her through any worries and trauma.

To my surprise, she was thrilled. As we ascended and reached greater heights with everything below so miniature, she was delighted. I blew a sigh of relief and took in this moment to remember. I was seeing my daughter experiencing the flight for the very first time. I'd lost many moments this past year due to Casey's actions and behaviour. It is something new in our lives, which can't be taken away. A step forward in our adventures and being together.

I gave Jessie sweets to help her when her ears popped. She felt some discomfort but nothing disturbing. Almost felt silly for worrying. Attention then turned to the views outside the window. She was comparing clouds to real-world objects such as elephants. She was mesmerised. I bought the iPad with me for her entertainment. By the time she got around to using it, we were already arriving home. The flight lasted less than an hour. Ridiculously short compared to our usual 5-hour travel by car.

The landing wasn't smooth. With much turbulence as we reached the runway, the plane was rocking and sliding. I had a genuine fear that we come off the track. Never showing Jessie my worries, she was oblivious to what could happen and just taking it all in her stride. An enjoyable experience together that we will cherish and remember. A new stage in our quest to bridge the gap between the vast distance between us.

32

CAFCASS OFFICER

During the January court hearing, there was mention of a new CAFCASS officer assigned to the case. The disruption is disturbing and it's unknown what information the newly appointed officer will have from the previous recordings. Everything is up in the air. Almost a year on from when Jessie was abducted, it feels as though we're back to square one and having to do it all over again.

I hate repeating myself, especially when I have put so much effort into the case already and provided so much information. It's not a case of forgetting as I remember everything. Doesn't take long to recite the truth. The issue is figuring out what information they have and what's missing. For the court to continue with so much information, not on file would be devastating.

Early signs are that this isn't going to go well. I've tried to connect with the new officer; however, she is challenging to reach. Jasmin was very approachable. When we did finally manage a convenient time to talk on the telephone, it didn't go well at all. It became blatantly apparent that she had spoken to Casey first. Sandra was already manipulated by her lies and ability to pass off her vulnerabilities as that of a victim. I was already being viewed as an abuser without an opportunity to state my version of events.

I tried in vain to discuss my concerns, but I was rebuffed time and time again. Eventually, my frustrations came to the surface. The ignorance that was being demonstrated to me was harsh and unfair. An outburst ensued when I became firm and agitated. I demanded that Sandra question Casey on why she decided to relocate so far away up north. Her response was very one-sided.

"She's already made it clear why she relocated. She was abused." Sandra said as a matter of fact.

I laughed, "She was never abused. She's selfish and made the kids leave the life they loved to be with Connor. Almost a year on and not shown one piece of evidence to back-up anything she said. I have hundreds of pages of messages showing how caring I was to her."

My pleas were falling on deaf ears. Sandra indicated that the call had elapsed too long as we had spoken for around an hour. It is confirmed that she will call me again shortly to discuss things further. Casey was getting home visits from the previously assigned officer and now Sandra. No-one has made any effort to visit me in person even though I make it clear of my availability. It's biased and unfair. I'm disgusted by the entire process. How can someone claim abuse? Never provide any evidence and yet people fall over themselves to assist and look down so strongly at the accused. They should be ashamed of themselves.

Sandra never did call me again, nor visit. Telephone calls were ignored. While I was firm on the telephone when we spoke, I was never rude. It's not going to be a fair assessment. My only hope was that she would get copies of Jasmin's files and realise for herself the contradicting behaviour of Casey.

My sister Shelly has a friend who's partner works in child welfare. When she shared some of the details to him, he was shocked and pointed out the many failings of CAFCASS to date. I made notes to use these points when I inevitably must contest her decision. It's been a shamble.

CAFCASS FAILINGS
- **Need to assess Jessie with her father.**
- **Wrong to have interviewed me at court. It was unfair after a stressful day in court. I was too emotional.**
- **Need to visit my home. Photos shouldn't be acceptable. Can't rely on pictures.**
- **CAFCASS can arrange for an assessment contact.**

I was encouraged to await the final report before deciding to contest the failings. If it were to go in my favour, then arguing the issues can cause unnecessary problems. Knowing that I can't rely on Sandra to contact me, I emailed with updates. If she takes the time to read what I have to say, then at least I may be able to influence her decision even if it is unlikely. We had discussed Casey's therapy reports which she hadn't received.

I was exasperated. Beggars belief that she isn't provided copies of Jasmin's files. It's absolute madness. I had to liaise back and forth with my solicitors. They in-turn progressed the request for therapy reports with Casey's. Everyone was chasing around for something that CAFCASS should already have.

At the very least, Sandra should've gone directly to Casey. It's weak and lazy from a supposed professional caseworker. The reality is that it isn't a full-time assigned CAFCASS officer. She is an agency worker. This case deserved the absolute best and should be a priority. We are let down at every stage. My faith in the family court legal system was exhausted. It is farcical if not heartbreaking.

Jessie had visits with Sandra but no-where near enough. She wasn't comfortable and didn't trust her enough to open up truly. If the role of an officer is to deal with child matters and file a report on something so crucial than being child-friendly and approachable should be a priority surely. I'm just disgusted with the entire episode and the lack of professionalism from Sandra. She's been inadequate, and I dread to think what her report will include. Can't be much from me as she has barely acknowledged anything that I've said.

I had revealed throughout various emails the concerns that I had for Jessie's welfare while in Casey's care. The contradictions in Casey's claims and accusations. Her behaviour throughout towards Jessie. There were many pages of in-depth notes and a summary of some of the evidence that I have in my possession. I made it clear that I'm keeping some parts private now. Leaving it for the final hearing, but I wanted her to know the truth and revealed a fraction of the evidence that I have. In contrast to the nothing that Casey has, it should be obvious who has been telling the truth. It should be a landslide in my favour.

33

EASTER

Throughout March, Jessie and I had enjoyed our weekend contacts with flights home on Friday's. I mixed the travel up by driving back on a Sunday, so we have different experiences on those days. It was becoming part of our routine — a new way of travelling which Jessie embraced.

We had been looking forward to the Easter holidays. April's a difficult month for both of us. Around this time last year is when Casey caused all this upheaval by abducting Jessie and relocating north of the country. A lot of turmoil in all our lives. As April approaches, it's something of a relief to be able to make positive memories instead of dwelling on traumatic events.

The confusion was caused when Sandra didn't submit the S7 report by the deadline set out in the previous court order. Casey and I are due to file our statements soon. The problem is that our statements are to be in response to the report. Without anything to respond to, we wouldn't be able to provide comments. I've been dismayed by Sandra's inability to be impartial. Now she's appearing incompetent which is just as deflating.

After much persistence from both of our legal teams, a response was received. Sandra had submitted her report, but it is to remain private at her request. At this moment in time, only the judge is to receive a copy. Neither Casey, I nor our legal representatives are permitted to receive the report. This was deeply alarming. I felt strongly that finally, something has flagged on Casey's safeguarding checks as Connor still hadn't been thoroughly investigated. It then dawned on me that if there are serious concerns with his past, then Jessie has been at risk in his presence for the past year. This made me incredibly anxious.

Everyone was confused. Neither side could believe what was happening and there wasn't any indication of who had been flagged as a concern. It could only be on Casey's side as I had done nothing wrong. I have been doing my utmost to correct the madness that she creates. Maybe my persistence of sending the emails with notes on everything had finally paid off — a silver lining to all the chaos.

The court hearing wasn't until Jessie returns from her holidays. I am to return her on the day of court in the morning. Casey will need to collect her and plan for Jessie's care as she herself then needs to attend court.

We had a fantastic time with family. Oakley and Jessie had an exciting Easter egg hunt in my mums' home and garden. My sister Kerrie and her husband Lee were in attendance. It was a lovely sunny day, and they were so happy. I recorded them as they ran amok seeking out every egg scattered and hidden. They also did crafts making and painting. Very eventful and fun for them both. There have been some great moments over the past year, but this one stands out for me with Jessie and Oakley together. They miss each other so much. Cousins, though they are more like brother and sister. Best friends. It is lovely to watch them together.

A holiday filled with memories. Jessie didn't want to return to Liverpool. By her admission, it's boring, dull and everyone's miserable. She wants to remain with me and have fun. I told her that I'm still fighting for her. Never lose hope.

Imagine my surprise after returning Jessie to Casey and attending court. It transpires that Sandra's report had flagged me as a concern and risk to Jessie. It was disgraceful. Even in the report, she couldn't be absolute with her assessment. It was so flawed and absurd. Sandra's problem was that she couldn't understand why Jessie favoured me so strongly and was so dismissive of her mother. It couldn't possibly be Casey's negative actions and failings. It must be my fault. The judge had no choice but to react in line with the report. My contact with Jessie suspended yet again. The judge gave me a few concerned glances, hardly surprising considering the damning verdict within the S7 report. It's just another hurdle to overcome. I had many issues with her report, which I will address at the earliest opportunity. For now, I must respect the decision of the court.

It did break my heart, and I was in tears. All I could think of at that moment was Jessie. I struggle myself without her, but the thought of her receiving the news that she can't see me broke my heart. I made a point to the court through my barrister that a cessation of contact will cause Jessie more harm than good. Allegations against me shouldn't be taken as a given without any finding of fact hearing taking place. It would hurt her immensely, especially as we both endured so much heartbreak at the same time last year. While Casey had enamoured Sandra, she should have been focused on Jessie. My little girl was stuck in the middle of this mess and almost forgotten between the battles. I was only ever fighting for her. Beating Casey is just a consequence of having to fight for Jessie.

I made my position clear that I accept the decision of the court but expect an opportunity to contest the findings of the S7 report at the earliest opportunity. The next court hearing will be an administrative formality. A permanent guardian is to be assigned as a representative for future proceedings as Jessie's voice. Sandra will no longer be involved in this case. She was just a temporary agency worker. Sandra was clearly provided with more power than her ability warranted. I feel more content knowing that a real professional will be assigned. A guardian must be very experienced in such a role. Their ability can't be questioned. At my request, the judge granted my absence from the next court hearing as the distance and costs incurred wouldn't warrant my attendance being needed for a simple administrative hearing. I do however need to be available for phone calls with an assigned barrister if I am needed for anything that may arise on the day. If I have learned anything throughout this process, it's that anything can happen at any moment. Expect the unexpected. Nothing goes how you would expect. With that mindset, nothing will surprise you.

The road doesn't end here. There is much to fight and contest. Though it is a bitter blow and a huge surprise. I arrived with such confidence expecting the decision to go in my favour. Move a step closer to Jessie finally coming home. It couldn't have gone any worse. The decision is tragic.

The journey home was sombre. No matter how hard Shelly tried to raise my spirits, it wasn't working. I bottled my emotions as hard as I could. Inside though I was in pain, suffering the most painful ordeal. I just wanted to let it out and cry. Our world had been torn apart yet again. It was long drive home, and the tears came incredibly close to surfacing. I had to take Shelly home, which requires me to spend the night. It's an arduous journey going out of my way to her house and then venturing on to mine. On this occasion, I just wanted to be home, let my feelings out and then get right back into the fight. Prepare my mind and gather everything onto paper for the next round of this battle.

34

DE-JA-VU

The feeling of De-Ja-Vu is challenging to dismiss. After long and drawn out court proceedings, I had been expecting a final resolution soon. Now it's back to square one. No further forward than the day Jessie was abducted. Torment, separation, hard work, fighting and financial hardship almost for nothing. The only solace is that Jessie and I have seen each other and shared the love in our hearts with many memorable moments. No court or vindictive rival can take that away. For now, while the battle continues into unknown territory Jessie, and I can cling to those memories to provide at least some comfort.

My solicitors were perplexed at Sandra's S7 report. They immediately reported that she had been incompetent. The responses were so vague, and nothing was based on facts. She had taken Casey's word on being a victim of abuse and just ran with it into her decision. Meanwhile, Jessie and I have to suffer in the meantime while we try to correct the disruption she has caused.

Sandra remained as a point of contact until a guardian has been assigned. To say that I was displeased with her would be an understatement. She did, however, have the decency to visit my conference room after court during the debrief with my sister and barrister. They were polite but a bit reticent. I saw no reason to treat her with contempt. She'd made her decision based on how she interpreted information. I was never given a chance, so I took the opportunity to now have an actual conversation with her. There was no yelling or pent up anger. I was talking frankly with respect, explaining my position and the obstacles that Casey continues to place between Jessie and me.

By the time our conversation had come to an end, it was visibly apparent that Sandra was questioning in her mind whether she had made the correct decision. She naively expected Casey to be co-operative and support Jessie through this challenging moment. I took Sandra back to all those moments when Casey blocked our contact, refused to send letters and continually makes up lies. How could she be so confident that Casey will be respectful? History tells us otherwise. Casey had manipulated her with sweet talk and the vulnerable demeanour she likes to portray. It can win some people over. Certainly, worked a charm on Sandra. So much so that she never actually gave me a chance to have my say before her report. After court, it was just too late. The damage is already done.

I sent Jessie a postcard immediately after returning home from court. A birthday card would be shipped shortly after to arrive in time for her 8th birthday. Another birthday we miss together. It's hard enough for me to bare. Lord knows how much Jessie is suffering. Separation is incredibly hard on her. She craves contact more than anything. It's about time the court focused on Jessie instead of Casey. She seems to have a way of twisting everything into her show. I'm expecting that all to change once a guardian is assigned. Their sole focus will be Jessie's welfare. They will see through any dramatics people are playing, and then see through their behaviour.

A reasonably length-ed email was sent to Sandra. There were a few points of interest that I wanted to get off my chest. I made the point to her that for all intense and purposes, I have been the mother of my child throughout her life. It was I that was responsible for doing everything. Casey barely lifted a hand to help. I finished the email by requesting that she find out when a letter is likely to be sent from Jessie. It didn't come as a shock to me, but Sandra was taken back by Casey's lack of enthusiasm to adhere to the ruling. Letters weren't forthcoming. She had been too trusting of Casey and dismissive of me. She chose the wrong parent. I never place obstacles between Jessie and anyone. My only goal is for her to be happy. I wouldn't go through all this hassle for myself. I have an urgent dental situation which had been referred to a clinic in London. Nowhere near as far as these court dates and contacts but I still refused to go. When it comes to myself, I don't care enough. I would do so much more for Jessie than I would for myself. I find unbelievable willpower when she needs me. Nothing can hold me back. Everything I do is for her.

I will always give praise where it's due. Casey is great when the kids are sick. She rises to the occasion and gets involved. The OCD kicks in with temperatures etc. Better safe than sorry. When the health scares die down, she vanishes from being involved in their lives. I play with the kids at the park, provided their meals, walk to school, homework, and play. I don't dismiss Casey through spite or anything sinister. It's just the truth, I always pleaded with her to be more involved, but it never worked. She took it as an insult rather than an actual wish for her to join in with us.

The next court date is early May. Before then, the guardian should provide a position statement based on her assessment of the current situation. Casey and I are then to deliver short statements of our own. As the weeks passed, we were both in the dark as to when the guardian will be revealed. It was in keeping with the entire court process; delays and distractions. This was no different, but as contact had been suspended, I was more anxious to get everything set up as soon as possible. Delays didn't affect Casey. She had everything how she wants it; the longer Casey keeps the status quo, the more claim she has that Jessie is settled with her.

I had too much to say and wasn't going to miss an opportunity to convey my opinion on the S7 report. Without a guardian in place, and, no statement forthcoming, Casey and I weren't expected to provide statements. I, however, took it upon myself to produce a statement. I couldn't sit by and wait for everyone to keep up. My solicitors were initially reluctant as we had to follow procedure though there was a loophole in that the court order did ask for statements. While the judge could dismiss my account or issue a warning, at least, my voice would have been heard. It's worth the risk. Photos of Jessie and I together were attached along with a powerful statement. By this point, my solicitors had complete faith in my ability to write my reports. They would edit where they felt justified but for the most part, left most of my statement untouched. I felt by submitting the statement I had a won a small victory. Casey wouldn't see it coming. I always try to remain a step ahead.

35

MAY DAY

To everyone's surprise, even Casey's, I arrived in attendance of the court hearing. Although the judge had approved my request not to attend, it didn't sit well with me. I have participated in every court hearing to date. Never missing anything; court hearing, phone calls, and letters. Any time I am needed I am there, so I made a point to attend. The reality was that our request to the judge was just an emergency option if I struggle to attend. Only my legal team knew that. We had every right to request my absence, so we used the rules to broaden my options.

It was a good thing that I did attend. Jessie's new guardian Evelyn had made a surprise appearance. I say surprise, because right up unto the moment of court no-one had any idea who the guardian would be and whether anyone had been assigned yet. We were all still awaiting a decision. So here she was with a helpful and friendly persona. She was easy to get along with and seemed professional in her approach. It was immediately apparent that she completely disagreed with Sandra's report. In her opinion, contact should never have stopped. There was no evidence to suggest that I had been anything other than supportive of Jessie. Our time together was enjoyable, and Jessie thrived in my care. It was a godsend; finally, someone with a degree of intelligence could see through the nonsense and notice the truth.

There was still a problem. Casey couldn't help but again feel she is the victim. Of what, I have no idea. She refused to allow direct contact or indirect contact. The guardian's pleas were being ignored, which wasn't a wise thing to do. It's best to get on with her seeing as it will be Evelyn's final decision which will ultimately hold sway on where Jessie will reside by the end of proceedings.

Evelyn returned to my conference room with my barrister and sister Shelly in attendance. Between us, we tried to come up with an arrangement that Casey will possibly accept. Evelyn could see through Casey and her obstructions but wanted to try and start with a softly, softly. If it doesn't work, then she has made it clear that she will eventually force it through the court. At Evelyn's suggestion, I agreed that for now, contacts with Jessie would take place at Shelly's house. It's still more than 100 miles from Casey's and a similar distance from mine. I wouldn't be allowed to take her to my home. I reluctantly accepted, the obstacles in contact didn't make sense to me, but it's better than the nothing we have now.

The proposal for contact relayed to Casey. She immediately blocked it, standing firm on her stance of no contact. I was shocked that she would continue her facade of being a victim and using it to keep Jessie away from me. Evelyn wasn't buying it and losing patience with Casey. Talk then turned to order a psychological assessment of the family dynamic. It would solve the issue of contact if a psychiatrist were to give us the all clear. I expressed my concern at the added delay. It would take months to get the appointment, and then there would need to be time for a report. After that, a court hearing would need to be arranged. My barrister supported the guardian's proposal. I wasn't convinced but agreed to whatever they recommended.

36

PRESSURE

Pressure from Evelyn was taking its toll on Casey. She had been used to swaying everyone she meets. A sob story with no evidence, and the complete opposite to Jessie and I. While I haven't had the opportunity to present my testimony to the court, Casey was becoming aware that I do have proof of my support. What she doesn't realise is that I've had it at hand ready to produce from day one. Amazingly, the court has dragged on for far too many hearings and at no point has there been an opportunity to submit my evidence. The only way my proof can be produced is if there is a finding of fact hearing. It would be a chance for Casey to explain in explicit detail everything that she is accusing me. So far, it's been incredibly vague. Even I don't know what I have supposedly done, which causes her such distress. The other opportunity is the final hearing. Until either of those moments, I must bide my time, look on with astonishment at the nonsense claims against me. The further Casey digs herself in by making such grand and frivolous remarks against me, the more explosive her lies will be shown up with my evidence. I take the hits, no matter how many times just waiting for my chance to shoot back. It will be something to witness.

Casey had to submit her statement blind, allowing me to write mine in response. It was her one chance to produce a statement that explains in full detail all my infractions and the suffering she endured. Attach any evidence she must finally uncover me as a fraud, abuser, master manipulator, and narcissist. After all, that is how she has been portraying me from the start. It may be surprising to some that her statement while full of countless pages were yet again vague. The only evidence she supplied were copies of my social media posts after she had abducted Jessie. At a time when I was most vulnerable, emotional and most importantly, not myself. Admittedly, I could be forgiven for venting my frustration and showing that I am human. The posts weren't bad or harmful. I don't even regret my actions. The one article that caused Casey outrage was my re-enactment of the Jim Carrey court scene from the film Liar Liar. I edited it side by side alongside the icon himself. I demonstrated my anger and pain in that video. She wanted to twist it as me showing no respect for the court. After all that moment in the movie, Jim Carrey questioned the judges' decision.

Her statement was laughable. My legal team and I weren't expecting anything else. We knew that she had fabricated all of her stories and claims of abuse. When the time came to support those claims she was left in dismay. Now it is my turn to respond. I produced the best writing that I have ever written. Incredibly detailed rebuttals to her claims — point by point in response to her statement. Then I followed up with an acknowledgement of all the support that I had provided her throughout our relationship — supported by over fifty pages of private messages and photos. By the time anyone had finished reading my statement, the support I had provided couldn't be questioned. I had hundreds of pages of messages on file. I had to whittle it down to a concise list as to not irritate the judge. They have a lot of court cases and don't like to be bogged down unnecessarily by endless pages to read. My solicitors wanted me to reduce the statement size further, but I held firm explaining that I had been waiting all this time for this one moment. I can't respond with my hands tied behind my back. All the pages remaining are essential. While they represent me, and it is, of course, wise to do as they advise, on this occasion, I felt in my heart that I needed to submit my statement in its entirety.

I recounted moments where Jessie has told me heartbreaking stories of her desire to be home with me. The effect on her when contact stops, and we can't communicate. It takes an incredible toll emotionally. Everyone needs to be putting Jessie first in their decisions. She can't open about her feelings to her mother. Casey becomes defensive and loathed by any reference of me in their conversations. Jessie becomes upset when she must return to her mother. She hates Liverpool and the life she is forced to endure. It breaks my heart to hear of her suffering. A child should never have to feel such pain. Casey should be ashamed of herself. Everything that has happened from the beginning to now is on her. Her actions have caused everything. I am the one trying to bring normality back to Jessie's life. Every moment that I fight is for her.

The notion that Casey had been co-operative with the reporting psychiatrist last year was laughable. When I had read his report, it was filled with lies, exciting stories, and exaggerated emotions. She is incredibly gifted at acting the victim. Some parts of the report were so obviously flawed that I laughed. It's absurd that she gets away with lying. She declared herself as single throughout. Now it's been proven that she was in a relationship with Connor from the start, way back in April last year. To think, she can sit across from people and say to their faces that she is alone with the kids. At no stage has she ever shown that she can care for the kids without support. I did everything before, and Connor's come into everyone's lives and taken over where I left off. I don't think Casey has it in her to thrive on her own, and that is when life will get too hard for her.

There was an accusation within Casey's statement that I wished her harm and don't adhere to court orders. That hit a nerve inside me. I have deep hate towards Casey for everything that she has done to me. More importantly, for the suffering that Jessie has had to endure. I will never forget or forgive. I have never wished her harm, though, that isn't something that would please me in the slightest. When we were together, I told her on the odd occasion that if we were not together, then I would want her to be happy. That hasn't changed. Casey being miserable wouldn't help me sleep better, and I wouldn't want her to harm herself or otherwise so I was disgusted that she would even make such a disturbing comment.

Every court order I have followed to the word. The only incident was when she tried to alter the travel arrangement, and I refused to return Jessie to her dad. The agreement was for me to return Jessie to Casey. She dug her heels in, as did I. I never once refused to return Jessie to Casey. There were occasions when I did ask my solicitors of my options as sometimes Jessie was anxious about going back. Each time I was advised that there is no other choice now. She must go back, and to that, I returned her. Casey wasn't involved in those discussions; they were private and nothing more than a conversation.

37

EMOTIONAL COURT

28th June 2018, I arrived at court with Shelly in tow. We were in positive spirits. Spent the previous night at the nearby Premier Inn hotel. As always, when we are together, there are plenty of laughs. I tend to behave randomly and silly. It had the waiter amused. He'd become used to seeing us on an almost monthly basis as it's our go-to hotel for court hearings. As soon as he sees me arrive, there's a look of oh no on his face but in a fun manner.

Shelly and I bought that same fun energy with us into court. The only way was up for us. I was in the ascendancy. Contact stopped two months ago. I was fighting every inch to get it reinstated. The restrictions can't last forever. Progress was made at every opportunity. The pressure was on Casey to either restore contact or continue being difficult. Either way is hardly glamorous. To give-in and allow contact would be a loss of control to her. Keeping up her charade will only look bad in the end.

To my shock and horror, Casey and her mum were standing by the elevator. Not directly next to it, instead in the middle of the foyer facing the elevator. It was wide enough to walk past without being close to each other. Shelly and I ignored them but continued our conversation, which included us laughing as we often do. It wasn't to offend anyone. Casey's mum acted up, laughing randomly to herself as we walked. She just came across as moronic. I don't have any time for her and the behaviour she exerts doesn't have any effect on me. Must surely be for her benefit. Whenever Casey is around her mother, she causes problems. I knew that today would be a battle between her mother and I. Casey will follow her orders. The difference is that I am calculated and calm in a storm. Her mother thinks she knows everything but lies can't beat the truth. Today we appear in court with evidence from our submitted statements. I wish her luck in trying to dismiss my statement.

There's a small cafe at the end of the corridor past the endless row of elevators. To be respectful of Casey, Shelly and I walked over to the cafe and sat at one of the tables. I chose the chair that faces the elevator. In hindsight maybe it would have been less confrontational for Shelly to sit there. It didn't occur to me at the time. My only thought was that I needed to know when the corridor is clear so that I can go up to the floor of the courtroom and book myself in. Sharing an elevator with Casey would beyond awkward for us both.

To my amazement, Casey's dad had just returned from the toilet. That would explain why Casey and her mother hadn't used the elevator yet. He noticed me looking in their direction. Only he knows why he decided to storm towards me. Maybe it's the fact that I'm there at all or wasn't happy with me looking at them. I was genuinely only interested in the elevator.

I turn to Shelly, "Casey's dad is storming towards us."

"What's he doing?"

"I have no idea. We'll find out in a minute."

I didn't care that he was charging towards me. He's a big unit, solid and potentially vicious. When it comes to myself, I'm not too bothered. It's only when Jessie is involved when I become like the Incredible Hulk and find so much energy. I had done nothing wrong, so sat composed, watching him charge at me. Just goes to show the lack of restraint her family has compared to mine. We are the victims, yet we act with grace, poise, and control. Leave them to do what they want. Hardly looks good to be crazed in court!

Casey's mum quickly grabbed his arm. She had a quiet word with him, and they then made their way up the elevator without incident. It was an eventful morning. Out of nowhere my barrister, Miss Choi appeared to my right having bought a coffee from the cafe. I hadn't been aware that she had arrived yet. I explained the incident that just happened. She raised her eyebrow but wasn't too surprised. Miss Choi told that people have different ways of dealing with the stress of court. Doesn't help things, though to lose control. It's difficult for everyone.

The day was something of a mixed bag. Negotiations didn't get anywhere. It was hardly surprising with Casey's parents on the scene. They don't like weakness — bullies, demanding everything that they want. There's no thought for even a second of the children involved. It was going to be a battle of attrition. Neither side was backing down on their demands. I wanted direct contact re-instated to the same level before it was suspended. I had proven beyond a doubt that I am not what Casey has portrayed. How could contact restrictions be justified?

Casey didn't want me to have any contact. We were at a stalemate. Casey went on about the episode last year when Jessie spoke to her mother about negative conversations we had had. The only way to proceed was to have a cross-examination hearing to put the situation to bed once and for all finally. Shelly and I were more than up for it; we were ready the first time before Casey changed her mind at the last moment. Both times her mother was on the scene in court. Such a coincidence. I'm sure her mother had arrived to be disruptive, but I don't think she expected to get caught in the middle of this mess as entwined as she had become.

When we all proceeded to the courtroom, the judge was confused. He struggled to comprehend what was happening. By now he saw through Casey. We had started court proceedings last year with her hiding behind a screen. Blocks contact at every opportunity and now her lies are exposed. When a psychological assessment of the family dynamic was mentioned, he was perplexed. He made it clear that he has never made an order or recommendation of it and viewed it as a waste of time and money, considering where we are in proceedings. It was his view that there had been enough delays and saw no reason to prolong the fighting between both parents, which in his opinion will be more detrimental in the long run. There wasn't enough evidence (if any) from Casey to warrant a full finding of fact hearing. The order was made that we move straight to a final hearing at the next available date after the summer holidays.

Time will be needed to allow for the guardian to do a full analysis and report and then for both Casey and me to submit our statements. Again, I was to provide mine after hers. There would be the cross-examination of myself, Shelly, Casey, and her mother. Emma was initially listed as a possible witness too. The Guardian expressed strong disapproval, and the judge was very much against her enduring such an ordeal. It just demonstrated how low Casey was prepared to go to beat me as an alternative Connor was submitted to be a witness. The judge refused the request citing that the father will say that whatever Connor answers will be out of his care for Casey. I, of course, would have responded in that way to any of his testimony which made it a waste of time. Casey's mum wouldn't be happy about being a witness; she likes to cause chaos but then runs back and leave everyone else with the mess. She didn't appear in court last time. It will be interesting if she faces the court next time. Perjury isn't something taken lightly, and she knows she's lying.

A last-ditch attempt was made by Casey's barrister to squeeze in an interim hearing before the final hearing. It was a chance to disrupt as Casey wasn't prepared for a final hearing. The judge denied the request stating that there will be no more disruptions. It's been going on long enough. Jessie needs to know where she will be living so that she can settle into her life wherever she may be.

The judge couldn't order the recommencement of contact, even considering the findings. It's almost sure to the court that I haven't done anything wrong to Casey. The accusations against me haven't been proven. As time had moved forward, the focus is only on Jessie's welfare. I couldn't understand why our contact remains suspended. It was heartbreaking knowing that we would miss yet another summer holiday. All the progress over the past year was replaced with continued uncertainty for Jessie. I was doing well and making significant progress, but she doesn't know that. The only positive was that since Evelyn was assigned, they have had regular sessions together. She was being made aware of what is happening as opposed to knowing nothing.

After the debrief with Miss Choi, my mood was lifted although I was still discouraged about the lack of contact with Jessie. While waiting by the elevator, I could hear Casey crying. She was inconsolable, being comforted by her barrister and parents. At that moment, I felt sad for her and wished I could alleviate the pain that she was suffering. None of this was being done to hurt her though sadly it had to be a consequence of getting Jessie home. I don't know for sure why she was crying. I can only determine that the reality of losing Jessie had become real to her. Either way, it's not a loss. Wherever she ends up residing the other parent will get weekend and holiday contact. The difference is that Casey isn't as committed as I. She wouldn't travel up and down the country to spend time with Jessie as I do. I think she was being given a reality check by her barrister — the seriousness of the final hearing. Surely someone needed to make her aware that her lies and false accusations have been pretty much dismissed. She lied and has been found out. It's something she will have to come to terms. For now, she still has residency of Jessie. Surely that's something positive she can take away with her. The fight isn't over, and there are no guarantees where Jessie will reside.

38

GUARDIAN BATTLE

Casey was in the midst of a war with Jessie's guardian. Thinking about it, that's not surprising. Throughout everything that has happened, she has never put Jessie at the front of her mind at any stage. Evelyn is now Jessie's voice. She is fighting on her behalf. For her, it isn't about liking Casey or me. It's what is best for Jessie. At this moment, the priority is re-establishing contact between Jessie and me. The judge did leave Evelyn with the power to order an interim hearing before the final hearing if she deems it necessary. He has left it up to her to try and solve the differences between Casey and me. If matters can't be resolved, then he may have to intervene regarding contact. Casey is under pressure to at least show some flexibility.

Every option put to Casey declined. She wasn't even interested in letters. I don't know what goes through her mind. She is jealous of the bond, Jessie, and I share. Resisting it though alienates her further. It took a lot of hard-work from Evelyn to ease Casey's stance. Casey was worried about how she would be perceived if she were to weaken her position. She was worried that people would think she's been lying. Evelyn explained that it would show that you care, and that goes a long way with the courts.

Even though progress was being made, I wasn't happy with the limited options that Casey was offering. She was trying to be helpful on the one hand to gain favour with Evelyn and the court but remain able to disrupt at any moment. She suggested that before the summer holidays I should travel to Liverpool and have a session with Jessie in the company of Evelyn. Then after that, Casey would decide on whether to allow further contact. It wasn't acceptable. I flat out declined her offer. No way was I putting Jessie through any more turmoil. The next time she sees me will be a permanent feature in her life with no more restrictions. For Jessie to see me and then possibly be torn apart again was not something I would even consider. Casey only thinks about herself and wielding power. I immediately think of Jessie and how it would benefit or affect her.

While negotiations continue, I raise the issue of not receiving letters from Jessie with Evelyn. She dismisses my complaints as irrelevant. The priority for her was getting direct contact established. I could understand that a message in comparison is trivial. The difference, however, is that I've been dealing with Casey a lot longer than she has. It's easier to get caught up in something that seems progressive only to find months have passed with no resolution. A letter in the meantime would soften the blow. All I could do was keep probing for something. As an alternative to poking the bear in Casey, Evelyn took it upon herself to get Jessie to draw me something during their session. She then sent me a scanned copy with a promise of receiving the original soon in the post. It was nice to receive something from Jessie. She always pours so much love onto the page. It wasn't lost on Evelyn, as she commented that it was lovely.

Eventually, Casey softened her stance by allowing a phone call with Jessie. Evelyn emphasised to me that this was a significant milestone and real progress. Casey was losing the willpower to fight a lost cause. Whether now or at the final hearing. Jessie and I will be seeing each other.

The phone call was a success. It was great to hear Jessie's voice. Have a bit of banter and have some lighthearted fun. She enjoyed our time together as much me. I didn't realise at the time, but Casey had been fine with Jessie's mood and behaviour after the telephone call. So much so that she was ready to allow unsupervised contact. I would have a single weekend soon and then an extended period during the summer holidays. It was a breakthrough. Casey gets the praise and adjuration from Evelyn and in some ways rightfully so, but she didn't enamour me. It shouldn't have been such a battle in the first place. She had been hiding behind a flawed report which gave her the platform and reason she needed to stop us for as long as she did. Yes, I can't thank her enough for allowing the contact without a court order, but I can't help but feel that Evelyn has forced her.

39

SUMMER HOLIDAY

The summer holidays were a real treat. Having Jessie home was a blessing. As it was arranged at short notice, I was caught off-guard in terms of making any plans. I quickly browsed online for places to take Jessie for a couple of days. Not too expensive but eventful. For the past two years, I was supposed to take her to Lego Land for her birthdays. Those plans were quickly dashed when she was abducted, and the following year contact suspended. Now that I will have her home again, it would be memorable for her to visit Lego Land finally. I booked a 2-day visit with a stay over at a nearby hotel just 15-minute drive from the theme park. My brother David and his son David-James would accompany us. When I informed Jessie, she screamed with excitement.

It was a fantastic experience which she enjoyed. She enjoys building Lego, especially Lego Friends. The theme park had something for everyone. Even adults could enjoy more thrilling rides than basic kids attractions. To my horror, Jessie is something of a thrill-seeker. A direct contrast to me. I like to keep my feet firmly on the ground with a gentle swing. Jessie loves to be thrown around like a rag-doll. I struggled to keep up but did my best anyway. Now TV vendors were stationed around Lego Land providing free

Now TV sticks. I managed to procure three sets for each TV at home. Jessie struggled to contain herself as I went to the 2nd and 3rd vendor. She did do an excellent job, resisting the urge to say anything.

I bought Lego at the gift shop which made her delighted. The Holiday Inn hotel was a pleasant surprise. Swimming pool and Jacuzzi included as a perk. After booking in and placing our belongings in the hotel room, we all headed down to the swimming pool. Jessie enjoyed herself, but my brother David seemed to enjoy the experience more than anyone. He is making the most of swimming, something he hadn't experienced in a long time. The pub, work, and TV are consistent in his life. Nothing else fits in around that Rota. It was nice to see him smiling. When I say smiling, I do mean smiling. It was as though someone had pinned the sides of his mouth to the top of his ears. Jessie found it amusing, mesmerised by his buoyant enthusiasm. "He's so happy" Jessie enthused.

Casey had asked me to keep her updated on Jessie throughout the holiday. I did mention that I wouldn't want to impose on her life too much. She then made it clear that I could share what Jessie is doing anytime. It's not a problem. Throughout the holiday I sent Casey photos and text updates on what Jessie had been doing etc. There was no gloating, and I don't think I was doing anything with her that would be a reason to boast. After the holidays when Jessie was back in her care, she tried to use the messages against me — complaining that I was bragging and trying to make her feel bad. It was a massive surprise to me. The messaging was only done at her request. I was baffled, she is something else.

What annoys me the most is that Casey never raises any issues to me directly. I can handle criticism and work through problems. If she had an issue with me sending messages, then why didn't she say something? She set me up so that she has something tangible for the final court hearing. As it was, she was going in with nothing and hoping for a miracle. Now she has something new to twist in her favour.

Jessie told me of plans that Casey had recently promised, which has yet to happen. She is due to ride a horse, holiday and some other things of interest. My biggest pet peeve is broken promises. I would rather someone be open and honest with people and say no. Building up someone's hopes and then crushing them with disappointment is not okay. I never make a promise to Jessie that I won't keep. Always follow through. If there's something I can't guarantee, then I will tell her to her face. She often asks if she's going to be able to live with me. My response is simple. I don't know; I can't guarantee it. With an honest answer, she is aware of the reality. Better that than continued failure. It's rare for Casey to follow through on any promise. She's so stubborn and defensive that no one can say anything to her.

Throughout the holiday I had kept in regular contact with Evelyn. She was happy to hear reports of Jessie enjoying herself. We tried to schedule a contact together as Evelyn hadn't witnessed Jessie in my care. There would be a need to see us together for inclusion in her final report. Evelyn was respectful of Jessie and I having as much quality time together as possible. I offered to use our holiday time to go and visit her, but she remained firm that it can wait. A date was set in early September for Jessie and me to visit Evelyn when I collect her for our weekend contact.

40

AFTER THE HOLIDAYS

The journey north had been arduous and challenging to make punctual. I was almost late collecting Jessie. Getting into the middle of the city is no easy feat. The handover time overlapped the appointment with Evelyn. We needed to get to her office with haste. There was no time for formalities. Casey was trying to explain something, but I didn't have time to listen. I wasn't rude but firm in leaving.

When we arrived at Evelyn's office with my niece Tilly, Jessie couldn't help being a bit blasé about the meeting. It was evident that she felt comfortable around Evelyn. So much so that she would switch off from listening between conversations. Evelyn asked Jessie a few questions and made some remarks of her own. When it was time for Evelyn and me to have a one on one chat, Jessie and Tilly went to explore the building. Evelyn explained that Casey only accepted the contacts over the summer when she was asked questions about Connor. Before that, she was resolute in no contact. She mentioned how comfortable Jessie is with me and that we have a close bond. The conversation lasted around thirty minutes.

As Jessie returned, Evelyn made a big point about Jessie's accent.

"She doesn't have a northern accent." With a wink, she followed up, "That's important."

Evelyn's entire demeanour and language suggested that she supported Jessie's return to live with me. She even asked Jessie if she would like to know her recommendation. Jessie declined. Later, I asked her why she didn't want to know. It was explained that she didn't want to get her hopes up.

After trialling 'What's App' for phone calls, it wasn't working out for me. Casey argued that her phone signal is weak where she lives. It didn't hold up as I'd previously had no problems connecting to speak with Jessie. The problem I had with the app was that I had to look at Casey's face every-time I talked to Jessie. I'm sure she was changing her profile photo frequently for my attention. I ignored it as best as I could. The reality is that I want the minimum contact with Casey in my life. I don't want to see photos of her or hear her voice beyond the handovers. Jessie, of course, is free to speak about her as it's vital that she doesn't feel the friction. For my sanity, the more I could do to remove Casey from my life, the better. Whats App was igniting a fire inside. It had to stop, so I removed it from my phone and deleted the account. I immediately felt a huge relief and a weight lifted. It's as though I had deleted her from my life. That felt good.

I'm curious as to what goes on in her mind. All this bitterness and disruption only causes more instability and chaos. They are rendering an aura of hate amongst everyone. My family and I hate hers as they do us. Meanwhile, an innocent child is in the middle of this madness. I try to lower my guard. Forgive and find solace in the hope that Casey would meet me in the middle and return the gesture. Our child just doesn't come first in her thought process. It's sad but when I must fight back, I will. Kindness isn't a weakness, but if it is treated as such, then those abusing my vulnerability will find that I am resolute.

I can hold a grudge for a lifetime. For the most part, I love, laugh and be merry. Usually the life of the party. For those that have wronged me and primarily caused distress in my daughters' life, there can be no repentance. The only one I will forgive and that is with as much reservation as I could feel is Casey. I hate her deeply with every fibre of my being. Nevertheless, she is and will always be the mother of my child. We don't all do or say the right things.

In most cases, gestures and interpretations can have ill-gotten reactions. Maybe Casey feels her actions are valid. I can't get into her mindset as she is one of a kind. Well - there is another.

Casey's mother will forever be the person that I have the utmost contempt. Jessie has never taken to her, so I have no reason to feel obliged to forgive on any level. Sadly, families can't come together or at least have respect to air their differences. Instead so much is done behind the other's back. She never had the decency to speak to me about anything. She is acting pleasant and whimsical to my face. Behind my back, an incredible menace with a dark and twisted agenda.

My thought process often goes off track. I try my best to move forward and leave these people behind to the lives they feel blessed to have, while the people around them must endure turmoil and hell. I love my daughter more than anything in the world. Nothing will ever be enough to push me away from her. It does dawn on me from time to time that she is the only thing keeping these people as part of my life. I want to let them go and never see or hear from them again, but it's just not possible, so I must endure living in limbo.

41

A FINAL HURRAH

Circumstances changed within just a week of the upcoming final court hearing. Emma sent a letter to Jessie's guardian, pleading with her to keep Jessie with them. It was clearly, one last hurrah by Casey's mother. The contents of the letter detailed the close bond Emma and Jessie have. Emma's heart would be broken if they were separated. She only now realises the reality of what might happen should the judge decide in my favour. I'm not heartless, but I did laugh when the letter was read to me via my solicitor over the telephone. They purposely read it to me before sending so they could gauge my reaction. It was explained to me that I couldn't react like that in court. Even if I feel that it's not Emma's words, the court will consider it as coming from her. It would look rather cruel to be so dismissive of her feelings.

I know all the people personally. Emma has never been close to Jessie. She's always seen her as a pain and an obstacle in her pursuit for attention. Casey's mother is vindictive and will do anything to get what she wants. Manipulating a child to write what she says wouldn't even cause her to flinch. Casey well, I'm sure by this point everyone can understand her well. No morals or acceptance of her negative behaviour. Between her and the mother, it's not exactly out of the question that they could get Emma to do their bidding. My laugh was at their audacity to force Jessie's sister to write a letter which condemns her to a life she doesn't want. She will have to live with that decision for the rest of her life. Do Casey and her mother care?

It could be the deciding factor on where Jessie resides. Splitting siblings is the last thing a court wants to do. Presented with such an expression of love between them could prove challenging to contest. The one important note, however, is that at no point has Jessie ever suggested that she has a close relationship with Emma. Her letters to the judge and during work with CAFCASS officers and the guardian have demonstrated a fractious relationship. One of, continuous battles at odds with one another. In her ratings of people, I received a ten. Emma and Casey both scored poorly. The dog Timpson received higher scores than them. Emma's letter may portray a loving bond, but Jessie's version of events paints a different story. The question is, who will be the guardian, and the court believe?

42

FINAL – DAY ONE

The day has come for the decision to be determined on my daughter's future. Our lives and schedule of contact to be decided by a judge. Law, whatever the outcome will bind us. It's been a long time coming and a very arduous journey to make it this far. The time endured has been painful and quite frankly a shambles. So many mistakes throughout by the system it's embarrassing.

1. A guardian should have been appointed from the start and been able to witness everyone's behaviour throughout proceedings.

2. Regular visits with Jessie to determine her mood and feelings.

3. Abuse allegations should have been dealt with immediately.

4. September / October 2017 contact should not have been suspended. It caused Jessie emotional distress.

The past month had been very confusing. At one moment things appeared to be going in my favour. Confidence of a positive outcome was very high. The next moment everything changes and I'm up against it. Never knowing what way this court case is heading. I'm content with my own efforts and those of everyone that has been supporting me. We can't do any more than already done. No stone has been left unturned. Throughout proceedings, evidence has been slowly building to form my case. Statements have been detailed and insightful into our lives. The judge and guardian should have an accurate understanding as to the circumstances of this case.

Throughout the entire proceedings, I've had to remain calm amongst the lies and false accusations from Casey. At no point has she ever provided any evidence to substantiate her claims. She has been allowed to abduct our daughter. Accuse me of being abusive and never reprimanded by the court. Surely committing perjury, abduction and slander should have some form of punishment. What message does it send to others thinking of doing something similar?

It appears mothers have free reign to do as and what they want. All they must do to avoid punishment is to drag the situation out for as long as possible, so the focus shifts from what they've done to the present and future. The argument was also made to me early on by my solicitor "Would you want the mother of your daughter to suffer?"

It's not a point of wanting her to suffer. It's facing the consequences for the actions that she decided — ruining my life in the process and that of our daughter.

Jessie is a hostage against her feelings and wishes. Dragged across the country away from her family and friends all because Casey had a desire to reside close to her new secret boyfriend. She still denies this relationship even in the face of overwhelming evidence. At this point, no-one believes her story, but she maintains her stance all the same. If a new boyfriend isn't the reason, then what justification is there to relocate such a vast distance? I've provided insurmountable evidence which demonstrates the love and support I offered throughout our relationship. There can be no doubt that I have been honest and honourable throughout court proceedings. By all accounts, the judge has an immense amount of respect for me.

I've arrived for day one of a three-day court hearing. There's expected to be the cross-examination of both parties throughout the final hearing, including that of Jessie's guardian. I started the day in a positive mood, although the significance of these final hearings wasn't lost on me. I was positive but anxious. This is it. There are no more opportunities to contest decisions and fight another day. The fight is today.

The positive mood soon dropped as my newly appointed barrister was late for the court hearing. She was due to attend at 9 am. An email arrived on my phone from my solicitors explaining that Mrs Stanley is stuck in traffic. There's no knowing what time she will arrive. The pressure soon came from the court clerks who questioned me on my barrister's attendance and when she is expected to arrive. They were clearly under pressure themselves by the judge who hasn't been the most patient throughout proceedings. A comprehensive and particular judge. I don't always agree with his decisions though I do respect the position he holds and his dedication at getting to the bottom of everything. I know when decisions have gone against me in the past that it is based on his limited knowledge at a given moment. Had he known what he does now I'm sure those restrictions would never have been granted.

There's a serious risk that I may have to represent myself in my barrister's absence. A very daunting task considering the severity of these hearings: I'm not afraid to speak in court and do have a basic understanding of the court procedure, having endured many court hearings to date. Though, at such a crucial moment in proceedings, it was vital that I have the best people representing me. After all, Casey has professionals assisting her. It would be very unfair to place me at a disadvantage through no fault of my own.

A court clerk was distressed and motioned for me to attend the hearing without representation. Upon Casey's and the guardian's legal representatives realising the situation, they quickly stood the trial down until my barrister arrives. The judge was informed of the status. The worry though is that there is bound to be a limit to everyone's patience. The hearing must go ahead today.

I phoned my solicitor pleading with them for an update on Mrs Stanley's status. Explaining how close I came to represent myself. Their advice was for me to relax as it won't go to me attending alone. Just inform everyone that Mrs Stanley is on her way. She's due imminently — still no guaranteed time frame.

After much anxiety, Mrs Stanley arrived. It was our first moment meeting each other. Throughout most of the court hearings, I've had Miss Choi who has been with me from day one. I was incredibly disappointed when it transpired that she isn't available for these court dates. The process has taken so long to get to this moment there could be no consideration of delaying the hearings. I was instead provided with three potential candidates to represent me for the final hearings. All of which were very well qualified and experienced. I chose Mrs Stanley as she was more senior with superior experience compared to the other candidates.

Miss Choi was much younger. My guess is the early thirties, but I trusted her immensely. I didn't get the same vibe from Mrs Stanley. Her heart was in the right place, and clearly, she had made plenty of notes from the bundles of documents provided by my solicitors. I don't like taking any easy ways out. Fight to the end is my only way of thinking. She wasn't very positive about the potential outcome. I was annoyed, mostly because due to her lateness we don't have time to familiarise ourselves with one another. As always, I have much on my mind and plenty to say. Everything on the day was moving too fast. I wasn't comfortable and incredibly unhappy.

One aspect of court proceedings that I haven't liked throughout the entire process is the requirement for me to sit on the bench behind my barrister. I often have ideas and very good rebuttals to Casey's barristers. As I said previously, I'm like an encyclopedia of knowledge when it comes to this case. The professionals are great at what they do but they don't have anywhere near the extensive memories of what I know. Court hearings can progress rather quickly. Sometimes I manage to interject other times the opportunity is lost. It's a rather frustrating process.

Whenever I put my mind to something, I go flat out motivated with absolute dedication. Nothing has ever meant more to me in my life than resolving my daughter's future. I fight to make her dream come true.

The initial hearing was short, with a quick recess. All that was agreed was that Jessie's guardian would be cross-examined. After that, there will need to be a decision on what steps to proceed. District Judge Thomas explained that he has little powers to contest the recommendation of a CAFCASS guardian. Only on specific grounds can he overturn a decision.

I found the court procedure flabbergasting. It's as though the guardian is the judge. It's unbelievable. The court system needs to be adjusted regardless of the outcome today.

When it came to the guardian's testimony, it was nothing short of shameful. I have a positive relationship with her. On a personal level, she is a nice lady that is easy to talk to. I have no idea why she was saying what she said. It contradicted everything. I was made aware that she also had an extensive court hearing at the same time in the court building. She had to go from one trial to the other. There was also a requirement for her to leave early to collect her child from school. It was evident that either her mind wasn't entirely focused on this case or she is completely lying. She seems honourable and no real reason to lie other than to maintain her reputation. I guess that's something worth fighting. Though I have no idea why her testimony was the opposite of what happened, amongst all her responsibilities, I assume that she must have forgotten.

Months prior to the court hearing my solicitor had told me that whatever way the guardian decides, they will confirm that decision with as much persuasion as possible — every argument made against her decisions she countered. Even the judge was concerned that her reasons for supporting Jessie remaining with the mother were for Emma's benefit. She denied this, but the expression and doubt on her face indicated otherwise. It was apparent her decision was for Emma's interest rather than Jessie's who she's supposed to be representing.

Apparently, Jessie is too young to understand the significance of her decisions and how it will affect her life. It was utter nonsense. She's very mature for her age. It was her view that she would find it difficult returning to the family home without Casey and Emma. Again, this is ridiculous. By this point, Jessie had been home many times and used to having the house to just us. She embraced the tranquillity and being able to be free from arguing. It was a losing battle. The Guardian had made her decision and was determined to maintain her stance.

The one saving grace which she had little option to reply honestly was about whether Jessie had been emotionally harmed by the mother in her decision to abduct her so suddenly and relocate such a vast distance away from family and friends. The guardian admitted "Yes. She has been emotionally harmed by the mother's actions."

Bearing in mind the judge and guardian had nothing negative to say about me. All the negatives were coming from Casey with not an ounce of evidence to support her claims. The guardian admitted that Casey has harmed Jessie. Surely that's significant enough to place her into a stable home with me.

As the testimony was coming to an end the judge asked of everything that she had said which does she consider as the most significant. This was important as although much was said and questioned some of it was trivial and minor. If considering it as relevant much could be decided on frivolous things. It became obvious that maintaining a relationship with Emma and Jessie was important. There should be absolutely no obstruction between the father and Jessie. The relationship should be preserved at all costs.

Upon questioning from Casey's representatives of my potential manipulation of Jessie to the guardian, she responded,

"I don't think so. I've seen nothing that would suggest that. It's evident that Jessie adores her father and that he is incredibly committed to her."

It's a very fine margin between where Jessie should reside. The Guardian explained that it's her opinion that both parents can meet her needs, whether it be school or health etc. We had spoken previously during a meeting a couple of months prior. Her assessment was quite different. It was blatantly apparent that she was in favour of Jessie residing with me. She was even noting that she doesn't have a northern accent. It was her adding little things together to help support her decision to the court. In court, there was no mention of this at all. She had mentioned the accent herself, not me. It was just unbelievable.

It was evident that her opinion had changed initially from the video recordings Casey had forwarded to the guardian. She misunderstood the dates of those recordings. Thinking that they were recent, and the distress Jessie was enduring from contact with me. It's the same recordings that Casey had used to stop contact last year after two very short sessions. When I had realised the confusion, I informed the guardian via a text message. Her mind was already conflicted as she now imagined Jessie upset from our contact together. Then she received the letter from Emma. She had made her decision, which wasn't what either Jessie or I wanted.

So much happened in that courtroom that stunned me. I couldn't believe what I was hearing. Everything we had spoken about during our meeting appeared to have been erased from her mind. She couldn't recall anything my barrister rebutted. We mentioned how Casey only allowed contact during the 2018 summer holidays due to the guardian pressing her about a relationship with Conor. Now she apparently knows nothing of that at all. It really felt like I was trapped in a twilight zone. All I could do was watch on in horror. Shouting or calling out would do nothing to support my case. She's respected by the courts, so all I could do was take the hit and chalk off the loss. What I didn't realise at that moment was the significance of her testimony.

The court was recessed so that the parties can talk to their legal counsel in private. I was shocked when Mrs Stanley returned, providing me with three options:

1. Accept that Jessie will reside with the mother.
2. Contest the guardian's recommendation by cross-examination of both the mother and father.
3. Contest the guardian's recommendation based on the evidence already provided.

Mrs Stanley heavily favoured option 1. She felt that the guardian's recommendation was too strong to overturn. Her rationale was that it's not based on whether Casey was justified in abducting Jessie or whether there was abuse. It's that Casey is in the opinion of the guardian able to meet her needs now. I was deflated and incredibly sad. Ready with every ounce of my being to fight on and never stop. I don't surrender or take an easy way out.

I was being pressed immediately for a response. Shelly sitting beside me informed me that mum had said to fight on. The problem is that she doesn't understand that the chance of success is incredibly low now. In all honesty, it's impossible. When Mrs Stanley left the room to liaise with the other barristers, I quickly used that time to phone my solicitor. They have been with me through all the ups and downs. I don't know Mrs. Stanley. At this moment, I needed the voice and opinion of someone I deeply trust. Val had always said throughout that I need my day in court. I'm well-spoken and articulate, so she does not doubt that I would present well in court. Therefore, I was so conflicted. I've been waiting for this moment through proceedings, and now my barrister is suggesting I give up. Val told me to do what I feel is the right thing to do. If I don't decide to fight on, then she would totally understand.

When Mrs Stanley returned, she didn't look very pleased that I doubted her professional opinion. I was still on the phone to Val when she entered. I explained what she is saying and passed the phone to Mrs Stanley so that she could talk to Val. It was far too an important decision to take the first opinion. I needed to be sure. Mrs Stanley explained to Val that it's no longer a case of abuse and circumstances it's a welfare issue now. That changes things though I was utterly lost. She tried to sweeten the blow by saying if you go with option 1 it all ends today. You can relax for the week at home, and you'll save plenty of money as we won't need the other court days.

We were due to return to the courtroom at any moment. Mrs Stanley needed my decision. I was still undecided. As we left the room, I told Shelly that I'm going to keep fighting. I can't give up now. It just felt wrong to surrender. I will never give up on Jessie. It was heartbreaking. All that was in my mind was her distraught upon hearing of the decision that she would be stuck in Liverpool. She dreams of being home with her family to the life she loves. I can't let her down.

I couldn't understand why Mrs. Stanley heavily favoured the easy option. She's much more qualified than me to make such a decision, so what am I missing? As we entered the courtroom, I told Mrs. Stanley that I still don't know what to do. She asked the judge for a short break so that she can speak to me outside the room in private. We had a short conversation. She explained that the animosity between Casey and I would be less severe if I don't put her through the ordeal of cross-examination. The judge would also look favourable on me for not being confrontational. With cross-examination, it's almost like a lottery. There's no knowing how it will turn out. Will I lose my cool under constant false accusations? Will Casey become distraught with emotions. It wasn't a pretty picture to imagine. The odds of overturning the decision are negligible. Impossible.

Something else was also playing on my mind. I regularly recollected the insights from the psychic reading last year. Mum had recently bumped into Sal while shopping. She was informed, "It's going his way. Tell him to keep his mouth shut, and I see 50/50".

With that in mind and the crossroads I'm at, I was just so confused and emotional. Floods of tears consumed me. It was uncontrollable. Not the day I had anticipated. The only salvation I gather in the bad moments throughout all the proceedings is psychic reading. Even if it doesn't all come true, it's something to hold. To date she's been correct on a lot of things; Jessie being in a hospital, funeral, people underestimate me, Casey's in a relationship, a Jenny will come back in my life (though it's a Holly) and other bits and pieces. The only parts outstanding were me having custody of Jessie and meeting my dad. During the reading, she had said that court proceedings would be over in 6-8 weeks.

You'll have full custody in 7-9 months. At the time, it made no sense. How could the time frame be so different? Maybe for now this is how it's meant to be. In the future, maybe Jessie will come home.

I explained, "I can't do it - I can't give up on Jessie."

"It's not giving up. It's doing what's best for her in the situation."

"I just can't bring myself to say the words that I give up."

"If you end it today, think of all the money you could save to put towards the travel costs."

"I don't care about money. The only way I'll stop is when I hear those words from the judge. I can't say it myself."

"So. What are you choosing to do?"

"I'll save Casey from cross-examination and leave the judge to decide based on the evidence already provided."

"We'll have to come back tomorrow."

"Then, so be it. Hotels booked for the week anyway."

"OK. I'll inform the judge of your decision."

As my decision was passed onto the court, arrangements were being decided in response. While everyone in the room appeared to relax, I was questioning my decision yet again. No choice appeared to be correct. It felt like it was finished. No more battle. The inevitable verdict to be passed down by the judge tomorrow. Everyone in the room seemed to know the outcome already.

I waited for my barrister before leaving the room. I tend to think I'm whispering when most cases are that I'm talking slightly different with the same volume. I don't know if others, including Casey, could hear, but I asked Mrs Stanley whether it's too late to change my mind. I wanted to fight on. It didn't feel right inside to surrender after so long fighting. I hadn't come this far to lose.

"You've done the right thing. You really have." Were Mrs Stanley's comforting words.

Shelly was annoyed with my decision. The last time she saw me I had said that I would fight on, but I changed that stance. I knew that I had messed up. Mrs Stanley swayed me against my gut feeling.

In all honesty, it didn't matter what I had decided. Either way, I would have regrets whatever my decision. If I had chosen cross-examination and it didn't change the outcome, would it weigh heavily on me to witness Casey suffer? I don't like to see her upset, and it would've been too much to bear, witnessing such an episode and be powerless to stop it. I had asked whether I could finish the hearing if I didn't like Casey being questioned. Apparently, that would be contempt of court with very serious consequences. There was no upside to any decision. I took the advice of an experienced legal professional. Why hire her in the first place if I'm not going to listen. I had to trust that the correct decision had been made.

43

FINAL – DAY TWO

As I awoke in the hotel on day two of Court, there was a strange feeling of relief. The stress and anguish at fighting for so long were removed from my life. Yesterday was an incredibly emotional event. I was in tears, shielding myself from Casey by placing hands to the side of my face. I didn't want her to have the satisfaction of seeing me so distressed. The tears were for Jessie. I knew how much it meant to her to be able to come home. Live close to all the family. Come back to the life she never wanted to leave behind in the first place. I had failed to get the outcome we had both wanted. So much uncertainty in all our lives wasn't healthy. The constant fighting between both parents is damaging for all concerned. While not the expected result at least we can now plan our futures.

The relief I felt was an end to the uncertainty. We can now live our lives with more structure and understanding. Of course, the final decision hasn't been announced or decided yet. The judge still needs to preside over one more hearing. Today we will all know his decision as soon as we enter the courtroom. It doesn't take a genius to know which way it will be going.

I spent the previous evening working through many thoughts and digesting what happened in court. I finally understood why Mrs. Stanley favoured a less confrontational ending to this saga. It would've been a blood bath of emotions had we done the cross-examination. The thought of the Jeremy Kyle show popped into my mind. A chaotic TV show with dysfunctional families at war with one another. The image of that playing out in court wasn't very flattering. No good would come from that.

The reality is that I had submitted all of the evidence I could ever provide. While I may have presented well in court; there's nothing, I could say better than I had already shown. If the decision based on everything is that my daughter remains with the mother, then I don't see a different outcome regardless of how much more fighting is possible. At some point, one of us had to stop the fight. It couldn't go on forever.

District judge Thomas read aloud his statement and thoughts on everything that had happened. The one part that has stayed in my mind and which I appreciated was his mention of Jessie and me.

"No-one can be left in any doubt the love that exists between Jessie and her father and vice-versa. It's clear to me that the father's application to the court was made for the sole purpose of his daughter."

It was nice to hear the kind remarks and his awareness of the close bond of Jessie and me.

Following the conclusion of court proceedings, I had a debrief with Mrs Stanley and my sister Shelly in a conference room. Mrs Stanley put things into perspective.

"When you go to court you don't always get what you want. You do, however, get an answer."

It wasn't the answer I had wanted. Of course, I feel let down and incredibly sad for Jessie. We do have a solution though, and that's something we're going to have to make peace. The final was that Jessie would reside the mother. Holidays would be split 50/50, and we would both get alternative weekends. Exceptions were made for birthdays and important days such as Father's Day. We would also get a weekly phone call. It's the best outcome that anyone could get aside from her living with me. Contact couldn't be more often than fortnightly based on the distance and travel costs. In some ways, I think that Evelyn knew that Casey wouldn't travel as I do. Maybe she was right that their relationship would deteriorate if she were to live with me. Although it sucks for me with all the travel, this outcome probably is the only way for Jessie to spend time with all of us. She will be heartbroken as am I. It's been a long fight, with many ups and downs.

I was asked whether I would like to talk to Casey. My response was firm "No. I have nothing to say to her."

The reality was that at this moment there's nothing either of us could say to each other worth saying. If Casey were to be sympathetic, it would be meaningless and almost condescending. If she cared at all, she wouldn't have made us endure eighteen months of hell. For my part, I couldn't think of anything positive to say. It wouldn't do any good telling her how I feel and the disgust that resides deep inside.

It's best we don't speak. At least for now, while the situation is raw and emotional.

I made the point to Mrs Stanley that while I am committed to Jessie and will always be there for her the same can't be said of Casey. She won't even commit to any travel. Her response was that's an understatement. Even in just the two days accompanying me throughout court proceedings, she could see for herself what I have had to contend. Everyone that has aided me throughout has seen through Casey. She hasn't helped herself.

Even the judge provided her with a few stern glares. Witnessing him questioning the guardian the previous day and the looks across at Casey it appeared to me as though he favoured Jessie's return into my care. Sadly, after the guardian's testimony, he had little choice but to abide by her recommendation. It was explained to me that if he were to go against it, then Casey could be able to appeal the decision, thus causing more turmoil in Jessie's life.

Mrs Stanley informed me that when Jessie reaches 12 years old, her voice will hold more weight. She will be able to decide where she wants to live. That's still more than three years away with much of her childhood missed. Of course, we get time together but not on a regular daily basis. Casey decided to move so far away and cause the time split between us to be so low. It's very selfish, and 'her' actions will forever taint our life.

Jessie is my only priority. I will do my best for her throughout her life. I tried and failed to get her home. At least for now. On the day that she reaches the age of twelve,

I will apply for her to reside with me if it continues to be her wish. Should she become settled with the arrangements now in place and become bonded with her new surroundings, then I will behave in her best interests. A court application will only be made if it's her choice. While her remaining up north isn't my wish and neither hers, I will respect her decision if she decides in future to stay there. Her happiness is all that matters. She knows that I will always support her.

There were many failings throughout the entire saga. I just wish that the judge in September last year had been strong enough to order the return of Jessie into my care. He had been angry at Casey's actions in abducting her. She was only spared by her absence. A different judge presided over the following hearing which changed the course onto this drawn-out saga.

If the roles had been reversed and it had been I that abducted Jessie, there is no way the legal system would've allowed me to get away with what Casey has. Likely, Jessie would've been swiftly returned to the mother's care whilst the courts get to grips with the case. It's this lack of genuine fairness towards fathers that just must change.

Fathers supposedly have equal rights but that just seems to be a term used with little action to support those rights. Clearly, there is much to be improved upon, for everyone's sake not least of all the children at the centre of these situations. Their voices need to be heard more clearly and have more weight towards the outcome. Had Jessie's voice been heard with compassion and a support worker understanding the reasons for her feelings she would've been home with me. Like me, she has been let down throughout and no moment more significant than now. We have no choice but to move forward in life with the hand that has been dealt, due to other people's negligence.

The final hearing, in all honesty, was a train wreck. Had I had my original barrister with me maybe the outcome would've been different. I'll never know but things tend to work out one way or another for a reason. Right now, I don't know what that reason is. Considering the hearings were booked for three days I couldn't understand everyone's eagerness to get everything wrapped up rather quickly. I was caught in the headlights. Under-pressure to make decisions in an instant. No time to take in what's happened and reflect. I should have been afforded the time to decide. It hasn't been a fair trial at any stage. I just hope that the next father gets an equal chance at justice.

CONCLUSION

When everything had been said and done, I was rather frustrated and angry. I struggled to shake off the injustice. My name has been dragged through the mud throughout proceedings. The relationship between Jessie and I obstructed by false accusations. There should be consequences. I couldn't understand how the judge would allow his decisions to be manipulated by Casey with perjured statements. I had expected him to be furious. Family courts, at least this one was somewhat lenient on damning behaviour.

On the one hand, I would love nothing more than to get the justice I deserve. Take Casey to court for the slander, due to the defamation of my character. If nothing else she needs to learn and be culpable for her actions. It's been genuinely disgusting and abhorrent.

The reality though is that Casey is the mother of my child. Revenge would only harm Jessie. While there is undeniable hate towards Casey for everything she has done. My love for Jessie far exceeds that hate. Some could say love trumps hate. The truth is that Jessie trumps Casey.

I'll remain frustrated and somewhat bitter and as always placing Jessie before myself. I will nurture her and try my best to settle her into this new life. We have no choice but to adjust our expectations and desires. Enjoy the weekends and holidays. Make the most of our time together and maintain a consistent routine. While Casey can provide basic care for Jessie; she is an enigma. Hot and cold and lacking an emotional connection. Playing with kids is rare as is taking them out for entertainment. I hope that Casey raises her game and becomes the role-model that Jessie deserves. She deserves the best of everyone, not least of all her parents.

EPILOGUE – PART ONE

The ensuing few months had been something of a rollercoaster. Many ups and downs between Casey and me. She was using her position of power to be controlling as had been expected. There was plenty on my mind though that I needed to get off my chest. A lengthy text message was sent, which in hindsight went against my better judgement. I don't regret the content of the message just the act of actually sending. There was a need to keep it to myself rather than lash out. My thought process though was that if I'm ever going to say what needs to be said, then it's best done early. If bridges are mended in the future it wouldn't be appropriate on any level to open old wounds. It was now or never. Throughout the entire court process, there's never been an apology or any sense from her that she had done anything wrong. I wanted her to understand the effect her actions had on Jessie and I. The injustice and lies. I just wanted her to understand the suffering endured.

Casey was fuming. How dare I send her such a message. The legal teams had to liaise back and forth. Mine trying their best to douse the flames. They were disappointed in me. I understood what I had done wrong and apologised. In fact, prior to Casey's outrage, I had already personally apologised for sending the message. It wasn't done on impulse. I had spent hours back and forth contemplating whether to send or not. There was a threat from her legal advisors of a potential restraining order which I felt was an over-reaction. There was never any worry from me as this wasn't a pattern of behaviour I had any intention of repeating. It was a one off to get everything out in the open, so it doesn't manifest and causes me frustration in life. It was personal but at that moment I felt that it had to be said.

We had many issues to work through after court proceedings concluded. A lot of hate had manifested between us both. Trying to be kind to one another was just a facade. Deep down there was just animosity. Even Jessie had her own feelings and views on everything that had happened. She's the one living through the turmoil.

Casey was accusing me of manipulating Jessie. I felt that she wasn't putting Jessie first in any of her decisions. Never considering what is best for her. Just lies on-top of more lies. A cascade of drama with me the ever-predictable villain. Casey is always telling Jessie that your daddies a liar and not to trust everything he says. The problem with that is I can prove everything. Jessie has seen videos of us all when we lived together. Photos of Emma smiling and so happy. Apparently, she hardly ever smiles now and rarely laughs. If her life with me were so bad, it would be strange for her to have appeared happier during that time than no — just one of many examples demonstrating who's telling the truth.

The problem for Casey, which she never tends to grasp is that Jessie is very loyal to me. I don't ask for it and certainly don't influence her. She's just very protective. When Casey antagonises me or displays disrespect, Jessie inevitably takes exception to this behaviour. She resents Casey and has a deep level of mistrust towards her. While it's easier to blame me, Casey needs to temper her tone and be more positive befitting that of a loving parent.

An issue which Casey had been trying to avoid was now coming to a head. I need the tenancy situation resolved. She'd had control of my life for far too long. For unknown reasons, Casey was dismissive and obstructive to avoid removing herself from the joint tenancy. She already had a new home. It's fraudulent to be a named tenant on two social housing properties. There was no benefit by remaining on mine. Rather than make it easy, she was awkward. Both of our legal representations were moving on. Casey's had already expired as she was reliant on a public certificate which ended shortly after the court concluded. My representatives have been supporting me pro-bono from their generosity. It ends when they feel it needs to be finished. The managing partner was becoming increasingly anxious to cease representation as it was draining their resources. I was grateful for all the help but needed this last issue resolved.

Val tried valiantly to help with advice and finally, she drafted a letter which she sent to Casey's legal representatives. They responded that they are no longer in receipt of funding to represent Casey or communicate with her. Less than an hour after that response, I received a text message from Casey.

Casey: I'll be coming into the flat to collect my stuff with my dad and a police officer… or the other option is you give it to my dad.

Me: I've never had a problem giving stuff back. All you've had to say is what I've missed. I don't want you back at the flat. I don't come to your home. If you give me a list of everything you want that I forgot or missed out, then I will have it ready by the door for your dad to collect. I'm not permitting access to come in… I've tried to sort this for over a year.

Casey: I can enter the property. I will collect my stuff… I think I will just come to the flat to get the stuff with the police officer and my dad. If it's mine, I will be taking it. Then when that's done, we will have nothing to say unless it's about raising Jessie.

By this point, I was fuming. I spoke to my family, housing officer and solicitors. It was expressed to me that I can prevent her dad from entering the property, but as Casey is a named tenant, I can't prevent her access. The police will only be in attendance to make sure nothing happens between us rather than have any say on property. My solicitors suggested that it's best dealt with the police in attendance then Casey can't make up stories. When it's done, it's finished, and I can move on. They did feel strongly that Casey doesn't even want to come to the property. She is just provoking me to get a reaction. I took the advice on board and relaxed my stance.

Me: Please provide a list of those items you say are remaining at the flat. I will arrange for them to be ready for collection. Otherwise, if you insist on coming with the police that's fine too. Whatever you prefer.

My attention then turned to Jessie's arrival for the Christmas holidays. I had agreed with Casey a month prior that she can bring her via train to Chelmsford. It helps her as Emma is also travelling to stay at her dad's for the holidays. My patience was running out though as time was drawing near. Less than a week away from the arrival date and no information provided. I had no idea what time etc. Or the return arrangements.

Me: If you could provide a time that Jessie is to arrive on Friday and the date, time and collection for your dad to return her it would be helpful thanks.

An entire day had passed without any response from Casey. It's not acceptable to be in a situation whereby I'm waiting on the day of arrival for an update on when to expect Jessie. Casey only seems to respond to force. She grabs any opportunity to walk all over me as she does Emma's dad. I refuse to be made a fool, though. A deadline is now being set. If I don't receive a response, I will travel to Liverpool myself. It's an arduous journey, but it's something I regularly do anyway. Casey rarely helping just once or twice doesn't assist me very much. Jessie prefers travelling in the car with me anyway. I'd rather not travel if it can be helped though.

Me: If I don't receive confirmation of the travel arrangements by 10 pm Wednesday I will proceed as originally directed within the court order and collect Jessie myself on Friday 21st at noon… If you could let me know your travel arrangements, I would be most grateful.

Casey: You already agreed to the 21st so look back at your messages if you want to travel to Liverpool on the 21st, by all means, do so but Jessie will be in Chelmsford via train with me as already mentioned in a previous message. If you would like a screenshot of that message and you writing okay to it then I will arrange that with my solicitor… Don't give me deadlines pressuring me won't get results. Once I know exact times, I will try my best to let you know asap. Have a lovely day.

Me: Read our messages and look back at your behaviour. How can you not know when you are arriving? I haven't got angry you have. My solicitor told me to send that text and to take the court order with me on the Friday. If you're not there, then the police will deal with the court order violation. Or you could stop playing games and update me with the information. The 10 pm deadline is real. Your the one always playing games. I ask to be informed.

Casey: Again once more. When I get my tickets either tomorrow or Thursday at the latest as my dad is paying I will let you know the times. You agreed already for me to bring Jessie to Chelmsford. My plan if goes well will be to arrive at 5pm. Once I know more I'll tell you. Also waiting on confirmation from my dad as to what time he can meet me. Can't be any clearer than that or do you need me to explain further?

Me: That's all you had to say, Casey. You usually book plenty in advance as it's cheaper. Thank you. I hope we can both have a good Christmas and stop fighting each other. I appreciate you updating me.

Casey: I'll be there at 16:30 on Friday 21st December. I don't know what day my dad is taking Jessie back until Friday due to his work rota. All I know is it will be either the 28th or the 29th in the morning. When I know I'll let you know when I get a chance... regarding my stuff you have 2 video cameras, dads ladders, Emma has some things and mums Christmas tree. If the tree is up we can sort it out later. Bring as much as you can. There is absolutely no way all of my stuff has been given back. Do not drag Jessie into this Steve.

Me: I don't drag Jessie into stuff. All I ever wanted is for her to be happy. You knew before you took her that she never wanted to leave. That hasn't changed in her mind. In court, she never once changed her mind or be indecisive.

It's not my doing. It's her true feelings. You might not like it but that's the truth. Imagine your mum doing that to you. You'd miss your dad and you wouldn't like your mum very much for it. Wouldn't be your dads' fault... I've bagged everything up. I'll bring them with me

Casey: Don't get Jessie involved in anything involving adult matters. She's 8 years old and doesn't need to know everything... anyway like I said once I know what day my dad can drop her back in Liverpool, I will let you know as soon as I get the chance.

Another war had started between us. We're both very stubborn and feel disrespected. Events tend to escalate rather quickly between us though on this occasion; cool heads managed to prevail. The issue regarding the tenancy continues to plight us. It was so avoidable. I had been asking nicely throughout the past year for Casey to remove herself from the tenancy. I'd returned most of hers and Emma's belongings during that time. As the court has concluded, it should have been addressed immediately. I was left with no choice but to escalate the situation to get it resolved once and for all.

It was evident that she was lashing out at me. Not happy that I'm escalating the situation further into yet another court case. I had sent her a reasonable text message a few weeks prior just asking her to remove her name from the tenancy. I did at the time indicate court as a last resort which I would wish to avoid and not even sure if I can afford the application. She never responded. I had little choice but to now seek legal counsel.

I handed the letter to Casey. The contents served her with ten days' notice to remove herself from the tenancy; otherwise, I will be applying to the courts. Within any application, I will be requesting that she be liable for all the costs incurred. It seemed to have worked as the tenancy was eventually signed over to me. The saga had come to an end, and now there was an opportunity for peace. No more reasons for us to be at war, move forward with our own lives.

It's taken me a long time to see the truth and accept something deep down that I never wanted. Against my better judgement, I always felt that Casey loved me. Naivety, yes, for sure. That was my weakness. My kryptonite. I see more clearly now, all the events throughout our relationship. When our relationship started, she was in dire need of comfort, support and in some respects, a role-model to inspire her to be the best version of herself. For a while, that was me. As has been the case with many people in her life, there was to be an expiration date of my usefulness. When my value to her dropped, she was quick to react seeking solace from other people even if it meant being devious. She would go onto cheat on me and yet again towards the end of our relationship.

Casey is the master of manipulation. Any argument we have she quickly turns the tide, labelling me as an abuser. A cowardly response so that she can feel a victim and innocent of her harmful behaviour. It's sad that in her mind she has turned our entire relationship into something it wasn't. I loved her dearly, but by the end, the stress of her behaviour took its toll. She makes me second guess myself and wonder if everything I hold dear is just a lie.

I'm big enough to hold my hands up when I do wrong or go too far and do apologise. Casey has never apologised for any of her actions or behaviour. In her mind she can't do anything wrong, it's always someone else's fault. The one thing to take from that is that I can grow, learn from experience and be a better me for tomorrow. Casey will always remain the same person she is today and was yesterday. Tomorrow it will be someone else's fault. The cycle will continue.

As time moves on and we all adjust to the new life that we have been provided, I can't help but miss the court hearings. It was challenging and emotionally draining. Gathering evidence and re-living all our family moments, knowing that it will never be the same again was heartbreaking. I think what I miss is the hope for change. While the court was active, even the low and obstructive moments were only temporary. There was always hope and an opportunity to fight on and improve outcomes. Now everything is so final and not how I wanted or envisaged. The result is unjust. It's not fair for Jessie or I. Life is challenging and unpredictable. What sort of message does it send to Jessie? I struggle to find a positive to educate her on how this became to be. It's illogical, a liar and manipulator have everything she wanted. We are the victims that are stuck in limbo.

I had loved, cherished and trusted her with all my being. For that, I was betrayed and on the grandest scale possible. Not only did I suffer the heartbreak of the ending of our relationship but the forceful removal of my daughter. The person I hold dearest in my life. To do that to someone you'd have to be almost sole-less. Never to apologise or accept any responsibility of such an act is the actions of a narcissist. I remain committed to my daughter. I've accepted the hate her mother has for me. Where it comes from only, she knows. I certainly won't be wasting any more of my time wondering or trying to understand.

EPILOGUE – PART TWO

After countless provocation from one another, calmness began to take place. We'd both been battling for so long that it had consumed us. It took time to get to a place in our lives where the fighting receded. We'll never be best friends of course or hardly anything of a friendship. More of an unsaid peace pact. Nothing good comes from constant fighting. We all lose; there are no winners. It's something that we've both learnt along the way.

To truly bury the hatchet, I made a respectful offer to Casey. Should she or Emma ever need to travel to Chelmsford when I'm collecting Jessie. Then they would be welcome to travel the journey back with us in the car. I understand the difficulties in travelling such a vast distance.

It's certainly not easy for me. Consumes an entire day just driving back and forth. It's exhausting not only on the mind but the body too. Some journey's cause me to get cramp in my legs, which I have no choice but to endure. The worst part is that our weekends together are significantly reduced due to travel. We barely get quality time together on Friday or Sunday. Had she resided nearby we would gain so much. As it is, we suck it up and cherish the moments together.

The court order only specified telephone contact for Casey when Jessie is in my care for an excess of seven days. I don't believe that there should be obstacles between a child and a parent. I offer Casey to have telephone calls with Jessie whenever she likes. It's important that Jessie isn't burdened by feeling any animosity between her parents. She's becoming more comfortable with her surroundings in Liverpool during our weekly telephone calls. Jesssie used to stay on her bed or in the kitchen. Now she roams freely around the family home with confidence speaking to me in the company of others.

Casey has placed Jessie into various extra-curricular clubs outside of school. I don't agree with her choices, but I don't get involved either. Saying something will only cause us to explode again. The fuse is so finely balanced. The slightest spark could cause chaos. It's been suggested by Jessie that her mother has signed her up for boxing, kick-boxing and other clubs to address her pent-up anger. I don't want her doing combat sports, and it isn't something she desires herself. She would like to do horse-riding etc.

I feel that rather than Casey personally discuss and address the issues plighting Jessie, she is merely throwing her into anything in the hope of a resolution. It won't solve the underlying problem of Jessie wishing to reside with me close to the family she adores. The mistrust she has of Casey and Emma. With nurturing and support, their relationship can recover and thrive. She needs consistency, attention and more understanding from her mother.

Only time will tell how this story will end. I hope and dream of a love filled life for Jessie. That's all I've ever wanted. She knows that I am always there for her. I am never failing to be there when I can. One day she will be all grown-up. I can't wait to see the women that she becomes.

For now, I cherish her youth and love the person she is today. It has been some journey. There's only one person in the world that I would go through all of this for - my daughter Jessie.

FINAL THOUGHT

It's often easy to forget the delicate feelings of people involved between the ensuing drama and chaos. The friendships or love that once existed. Easier to feel hate than embrace love. Love requires vulnerability, whilst hate is much simpler. A lack of empathy, though isn't a good trait to carry around. Understanding the bigger picture and considering the feelings of others provides a better outlook on the current circumstances and the future. The only way to truly move on in life is to forgive and remove any burden of guilt or hate. If it's too hard to forgive, then move forward care-free but don't waste time on the past. The past can't be re-written. It's permanently confined to history. A positive future requires one to be positive in thought and actions.

APPENDIX

DIARY OF EVENTS

April 2017 - Abduction, phone calls to the police, appointed solicitors, accusations from Casey's mother over the phone to mum regarding alleged abuse of Emma, psychic reading and missing Jessie's birthday.

May 2017 - Offered the shared tenancy flat to Casey, staked-out Casey's parents' home, updated the school & education authority of the current situation.

June 2017 - Casey's appointed solicitors got in contact with my solicitors, nasty letter received from her solicitors and my court application.

July 2017 - 1st Court hearing, urgent next hearing ordered, no letters received, apparently Jessie didn't want to communicate with me, and Casey was too busy.

August 2017 - Conversation with a CAFCASS officer, urgent hearing arranged by the officer, no letters from Jessie though I was sending regularly.

September 2017 - 2nd Court hearing, the judge came close to sending Jessie home to me! Jessie admitted to hospital with thumb injury requiring surgery, two contacts with Jessie (3hr & 5hr), contact suspended!

October 2017 - Contested court hearing, Casey agrees for contact to recommence, so she doesn't have to be cross-examined, I stop further video recordings from being permitted, Jessie visits home for a short period to see my stepdad. Casey surprises me with a phone call during handover, arranges to meet, we couldn't agree on where Jessie would live, my stepdad died.

November 2017 - Jessie mentioned Connor, Casey lied to a psychiatrist about her life and played down her mental health issues, stepdads funeral.

December 2017 - Psychiatrist report, Christmas with Jessie and Casey's sister visiting.

January 2018 - CAFCASS officer taken off of case moments before S7 report to be filed, court hearing, Casey forced to commit to travelling at least once per month.

February 2018 - Half-term with Jessie. Travelled by plane after the holidays.

March 2018 - Weekend contacts, submitted a statement for court. S7 report was submitted to court but was withheld from both parties due to safeguarding concerns. I was convinced something had been flagged regarding Connor. I was shocked to find that I was the concern.

April 2018 - Brilliant Easter holiday with Jessie and family. She had a great time and really wished to stay longer. Returned for court only to have contact suspended yet again based on the S7 report by a newly appointed CAFCASS officer. She didn't listen to me at all. Stating the mother has already explained her reasons for abducting were due to abuse. She was so narrow-minded that she wouldn't look past her lies. Took her words as fact.

May 2018 - Guardian was assigned and wanted the re-commencement of contact. Casey refused. The judge was confused. He was surprised by Casey's stance referring to the hearing last October. There was a chance then to get to the bottom of abuse etc.. He thought we had moved on from that. Now we need to contest yet again. The Guardian made the point to me that Casey will be bound by law to disclose where she was staying on those weekends away when she was abandoning the kids prior to the abduction. determined to get contact moving forward. The guardian did mention a psychologist assessment of the family dynamic. Each person interviewed separately.

June 2018 - Court hearing, went my way with a final upcoming hearing at the next available date. The judge knew nothing of a psychologist and saw no benefit in dragging on proceedings any further. There was nothing in the evidence which would warrant a finding of fact regarding abuse as Casey failed to provide any evidence at all. Simply providing social media posts during the months after abducting the kids. They simply showed the effect her actions had on me rather than any negative behaviour. She didn't prove anything whilst I provided 50 pages of detailed message history between us which showed all the love and support, I provided. Separate photo collages of me with Casey, Emma and various dogs were attached. She had tried to portray me as an abuser of animals too. It was shocking.

July 2018 - Contact resumed thanks to CAFCASS intervention. Casey was reluctant to allow contact offering the bare minimum. She failed to submit her statement.

August 2018 - Spent half of the holidays with Jessie. Casey apparently didn't do anything with her apart from providing plenty of false promises. I took her to Lego Land for two days amongst other things. Provided Casey with updates as requested. Casey's statement again failed to arrive.

September 2018 - Meeting with the guardian. Casey's statement was submitted which included complaints of me boasting about the holiday contact which was shocking as I only provided updates throughout as requested. She had always shown appreciation of the messages.

October 2018 - Court concludes with CAFCASS favouring the mother only due to Emma's letter though wouldn't accept that being the reason, Jessie to live with the mother, the judge didn't want to impose too many rules hoping we would communicate well without the need for interference. Within one-week, Andy had moved in with Casey. Emma was rude to Jessie. Jessie was incredibly disappointed with the court's decision.

PSYCHIC READING

Court Duration - Expected to complete in 6-8 weeks.

Custody - Full custody of Jessie in 7-8 months.

Funeral - There will be a funeral.

Hospital - Jessie will be in the hospital.

Control - Everything's going on around me whilst I can't control anything that's happening.

ACKNOWLEDGEMENTS

The support I have around me has been wonderful. I couldn't be more grateful to my family and friends and not least of all my legal team. Forget an image of people in suits; this is real people with families of their own. They are taking an interest in my daughter and the suffering endured and offering their services for free in pursuit of justice. None of us had expected the court to drag on. The support, though, has never wavered or diminished. I'm lucky and blessed to have amazing people by my side.

The burden ultimately falls upon my shoulders. As time goes on, my legal team, have other clients to manage but most of all they trust and have faith in my ability to rise to the challenge — giving me more and more responsibility knowing that I'm always on point and focused. I'm like an encyclopedia of knowledge when it comes to my daughter and this court case. Locked into memory are every circumstance, date and episode. Without fail, I know everything that has happened without having to pause and think. It's been an obsession.

At no point should my efforts be praised or applauded too fondly. The people that help make this all possible deserve so much recognition. Without my parent's financial support, it wouldn't even be possible. It's unlikely that I would've ever heard from Jessie again until she's grown into an adult. By then who knows what lies and manipulation she'd have to endure. Her image of me could've been very negative. Considering how close we are, that thought is rather sad. At no point has Casey shown any enthusiasm towards supporting the relationship between Jessie and me.

My sister Shelly has been by my side at each of the court hearings. I am taking considerable time away from her own family. I'll never forget the incredible support she has done for me. It should never be understated. She stepped up in my moment of need — a calmness and voice of reason when I felt lost and anxious.

David-James stepped up accompanying me on the long journey's back and forth to Liverpool to collect and return Jessie. A wonderful nephew was placing family above everything. The journeys were more bearable with the laughs we had along the way. True acts of selflessness consistently. It's been a blessing having him help with handover's when I couldn't bear to be near Casey.

The people who make everything tick and put such hard work in the background every day are Debbie and Val. Without them, this would've been a costly battle. The reality is that I most likely wouldn't have made it this far. Costs were constantly mounting. Casey was trying her best to bleed me dry. Not only are they incredibly compassionate but brilliant at what they do. Vast experience with family courts and refuse to be bullied by the other parties. They've had to listen to my torment more than anyone. They are living through all the ups and downs in this case with me. They went above and beyond. Humility is astounding, and they are the best at what they do. My trust in them is absolute. Sometimes we differ on the direction or what's appropriate, but inevitably, I always follow their advice. Listen and learn from those with much more experience than I. I'm emotionally invested. While to some extent, they are too as they took my case very personal. They were also able to take a step back and look at the bigger picture in moments when I was frustrated and not thinking clearly.

Friends and other family members have put up with my often depressive demeanour. The vibrant and best part of my personality was often hidden and missing. I have replaced with so much doom and gloom. My world and life were shattered though everyone took the time to listen and provide words of advice. I appreciate everyone around me and don't take anything for granted. My little girl knows that I'm doing everything possible to get her home, but she may not realise that so many people are helping me along the way. On my own, I'd be lost in my own mind. The torment would've consumed me into a darker place rendering me useless. Thankfully whenever I was down so many people would be there to pick me up. For that, I am eternally grateful.

A final thank you to the one person that made all of this possible. By my side every step of the way, lifting me up when I am down, listening to my problems as I hit rock bottom. There to pick me up. Helping me financially when I needed it most. Emotionally never giving up. Jessie and I both owe so much to mum. I'm blessed to have her. I may not show it often, but alongside my little girl, there are no two people more important in my life.

ABOUT THE AUTHOR

Stephen Bradley-Waters is 36 and lives in Essex, working hard to establish himself in a new career. After the ending of a long-term relationship, it was time for a change and evaluate his life. Writing has always been a long-held interest. Now pursuing his dream of being a writer.

The follow-up story, 'A Heartbroken Daughter' is OUT NOW. Delving into life after Family Court, and the behaviour of everyone involved a year on from the Courts decision.

Stephen continues to write and transform words into stories. In the near future he expects to produce fiction novels, and one day, a final conclusion to the 'A Father's Daughter' trilogy.

To find out more about Stephen Bradley-Waters please visit www.stephenbradleywaters.com

Printed in Great Britain
by Amazon